CU00722883

PENS, PROFILES AND PLACES

PENS, PROFILES AND PLACES

A Literary Tour Round Yorkshire

Marion Troughton

Smith Settle

First published in 1989 by
Smith Settle Limited
Ilkley Road
Otley
LS21 3JP

© Marion Troughton 1989

All rights reserved. No part of this book may
be reproduced, stored in a retrieval system,
or transmitted in any form or by any means,
without the prior permission of the
publishers.

ISBN Paperback 1 870071 27 1
Hardback 1 870071 28 X

Designed, printed and bound by
Smith Settle
Ilkley Road
Otley
LS21 3JP

Contents

Illustrations

Introduction

A square envelope addressed to myself at Filey in September 1950 — that can be classed as the start of my quest for Yorkshire's literary links. On the back of the envelope were a few scribbled notes relating to the portrait of Ellen Nussey donated by the novelist Eric Roberts and displayed in one of the rooms of what was formerly Cliff House in Filey, the house where Charlotte Brontë and her friend Ellen had stayed after Anne Brontë's death in Scarborough in May 1849.

During that early visit to Filey I was intrigued enough to set out and discover more of Charlotte's haunts, but was not too successful. One clergyman observed that he could hardly believe that Charlotte had stayed at the resort, otherwise 'more would have been made of it'. However, as I have since discovered, it is the case that much of the county's literary heritage has been neglected, and some surprising discoveries can be made in the most unexpected places.

From that initial visit came an increased interest in Yorkshire's literary past, one pursued on later holidays. For example, the novelist Leo Walmsley's 'Bramblewick', his fictional recreation of Robin Hood's Bay, was explored long before the now successful Leo Walmsley Society was founded. Many visitors to Whitby may recall, like me, the owner of the town's principal bookshop rightly recommending them to 'read Walmsley to get the feel of the area'.

It is often the case in a literary quest of this sort that reading one work leads on to another: the advice of a Middlesbrough school-teacher in 1951 to read the work of Whitby's Mary Linskill led me on to Mrs Gaskell's portrayal of the Whitby of whaling times in *Sylvia's Lovers,* and eventually to the work of Storm Jameson, who helped to put the town on the literary map as 'Danesacre'.

Over the years, magazine interviews with many well-known authors provided at first hand an insight into how writers often use their own lives and surroundings as the raw material for their work. Phyllis Bentley, Dorothy Una Ratcliffe at Temple Sowerby Manor in

Westmorland, William Riley at Silverdale and Sir Osbert Sitwell at Renishaw Hall were just a few of the memorable interviewees.

Over the years I undertook a great deal of personal research in pursuit of my growing interest. Many more explorations were made to places associated with literary figures and some difficult enquiries were pursued. Sometimes these resulted in little-known or largely unpublicised links with the more notable regional figures; occasionally the complete 'literary landscape' of a once-famous but now neglected author was uncovered and explored to the end of its topographical thread. All my searches and enquiries during what has been nearly forty years' work have been rewritten, revisited or reassessed for this book. The comments are thus based on entirely my own impressions, except where quotations are given.

What I have endeavoured to do is to seek out the less well-known as well as the more famous of Yorkshire's literary links, to illuminate some of the more neglected of our writers, and to show how the county has been portrayed through the centuries by novelists, essayists and poets. If the book sets other people on a journey of exploration to the places mentioned, investigating their own area's possible literary links, or simply a reading of some of the books mentioned, it will have achieved its objective.

This book is not meant to be comprehensive or scholarly — it would probably take a twenty volume collection to include all writers connected with the county up to the present day. There have been many writers who have had a passing association with the region whom I have not included as I have thought the links so slight. Similarly, a vast number of eminent topographical writers have been omitted, not through lack of interest or appreciation of their fine work, but just because of the vast volume of material.

At the end of the book are lists of places connected with various authors, and also details of literary societies who are always happy to welcome new members. Gratitude is offered to the secretaries of these societies for the details and also to the many other people, including the keepers of museums and literary homes, who have supplied extra details: especially Mrs Julia Monkman of Shandy Hall, Coxwold; Dr

Juliet Barker of the Brontë Society; and Mr Leslie Wenham, former headmaster of Richmond Grammar School who gave me details of Lewis Carroll's former school at Richmond.

Thanks are also due to many people who have helped with information and illustrations, most notably the staffs of the reference libraries in Leeds and Bradford; the Brynmor Jones Library of Hull University and the John Rylands Library of Manchester University who helped to provide illustrations; Hull Library who located more information about E C Booth; Mrs Janet Barnes, keeper of the Ruskin Gallery in Sheffield for her assistance regarding illustrations connected with John Ruskin and information about the Guild of St George; Miss Sarah Northcroft, assistant arts keeper of York City Art Gallery for her help with illustrations of old York; Russ Allen of Scarborough's Theatre-in-the-Round; the Rev R Cooper, Rector of Croft, for the pictures of Croft Church; the administrator of Castle Howard Estates for the old picture of Castle Howard; Miss M Seviour, research assistant at the Ferens Art Gallery, Hull, for her assistance with the portrait of Andrew Marvell; Miss K A Pitt of Skipton Library for the arrangement regarding the illustrations of Malham Tarn; Miss J Crowther of the local studies department of Hull Library for provision of the Winifred Holtby illustrations and supplying other details; to Paul Berry, to whom copyright in the Winifred Holtby illustrations belongs; and to those people and institutions who supplied illustrations and are acknowledged elsewhere. In fact, sincere thanks to anyone who has made the writing of this book such a pleasure.

Especial gratitude must go to Mark Whitley, editor, and Smith Settle, my publisher, for their unfailing help, guidance and patience.

A modern view of York's city walls and Minster by night.

York and Environs

York is one of the most rewarding cities in the country in which to seek evidence of a literary heritage. In this ancient city everybody seems so intent on their own kind of exploration, and one can undertake as much literary discovery as desired. Authors who belong to York, or who have associations with it and its surroundings, range from the anonymous writers of the city's famous cycle of mystery plays to modern authors.

Of the many places of great antiquity and beauty throughout the city, one of the favourite sites for modern visitors is the museum gardens and St Mary's Abbey ruins. In fact for many people a visit to York is incomplete without a stroll round the gardens here. During the quadriennial York Festival, visitors and local residents alike enjoying their walks will also notice the scaffolding, stage sets, tiers of seating and signs connected with the performance of the mystery plays.

York's mystery plays date back to the fourteenth century, and the complete cycle of forty-eight plays tells the story of mankind from Creation to the Last Judgement. From the first they were open-air performances — indeed street performances in the earliest days. Members of the various local guilds each gave their plays on moveable platforms in different parts of the city. Each guild was responsible for the provision of the moveable stage — the mediaeval streets were very narrow and often crooked, with houses overhanging the thoroughfare, making it impossible to use high stages — as well as the actors, whatever scenery was used, the costumes and any other props. The corporation, who had charge each year of the whole event on Corpus Christi Day (the first Thursday after Trinity Sunday), usually arranged the performances in eight parts of the city.

Originally the event began at four o'clock in the morning with the proclamation of the plays by the city herald. The whole sequence begins with the creation of the world, then carries on to the birth, life, passion and death of Christ, his resurrection and ascension into Heaven. Finally comes the Last Judgement, ending at twilight and signifying the end of the world.

The whole spectacle would have had a tremendous influence on the lives of ordinary people in the Middle Ages — a time of great fear and superstition — and given affirmation to their religious belief. Similarly the modern performances are a never-to-be-forgotten experience for those who now come to see them.

The plays were popular right up to Elizabethan times, but after the Reformation the performances ceased for hundreds of years, partly due to the church authorities of the time who disapproved of their displays of religious pageantry. All copies of the plays were collected for 'correction' and then disappeared, except one copy that had been on loan to members of the Fairfax family. This eventually found its way into the hands of the Leeds antiquarian Ralph Thoresby, and later still it passed to the Ashburton Library and the British Museum. In the 1880's Miss Lucy Toulmin Smith edited the York cycle, but no other work is believed to have been done on the plays until Dr J S Purvis compiled the text of the 1951 performances for the Festival of Britain.

Canon Purvis spent over three years translating the plays into a modern idiom without marring their essential qualities. In 1963 he told the writer something of their story:

'The description "mystery" is not of a miracle play, but', he explained, 'of religious plays performed by trade guilds. Such guilds were often called "mysteries" in the Middle Ages because each trade had its own secrets.'

He believed the plays to be the work of three men; the first probably a well-educated monk who planned the sequence and wrote the bulk of the plays; while later two others made additions. The original cycle is thought to date from around 1350, taking over eighty years to be completed.

The director on that first occasion in 1951 after an interval of hundreds of years was E Martin Browne, a skilled producer of

The crucifixion scene from the York mystery plays.

St William's College.

The 'Holy Family' from the 1988 production of the mystery plays, with Victor Banerjee as Christ.

religious drama who retained the position until the end of 1957. He believed that the performances should not fall into a set pattern, a decision that has been followed by subsequent directors. Since 1951 the plays have been staged as part of the York Festival in the open air against the impressive backdrop of ancient St Mary's ruins. The 1988 performances brought another innovation when the part of Christ was played by Victor Banerjee, a Hindu from Calcutta who has also starred in David Lean's film *A Passage to India*. Steven Pimlott, assistant director of Sheffield's Crucible Theatre, was the artistic director.

York, Coventry, Chester and Wakefield still have their own cycles of mystery plays, though those of York and Wakefield are regarded as the most complete. Canon Purvis considered the York cycle to be in the forefront in terms of quality and spiritual value, and they have been described as plays 'with a poetic beauty and grandeur of conception that places them in the first row of English drama and literature'.

A man who knew York in the earliest days of the mystery plays was John Wycliffe (c. 1330-1384), often called the 'morning star of the Reformation'. A tablet on the outer wall of the Minster, almost opposite St Michael-le-Belfry Church, indicates that Wycliffe was ordained priest in the building in 1351. He is believed to have been born in the North Riding village of Wycliffe, though some historians have put forward the village of Hipswell, near Richmond, as his birthplace. It is believed his early education was at Egglestone Abbey, Teesdale, not far from his home. (This is now a ruin.) After completing his education at Oxford he came to York and lived with the Friars Preachers until his ordination. He later returned to Oxford to become master of Balliol College — a position he resigned to become a parish priest. His first parish was Fillingham, Lincoln, but in 1374 he moved to Lutterworth in Leicestershire where he worked on the first English translation of the Bible, assisted by Nicholas of Hereford and other scholars.

Wycliffe firmly believed that everyone should be able to hear the Scriptures read in their own language, even if they themselves could not read. His convictions seem reasonable today, but were regarded as heresy in the fourteenth century. His New Testament was completed in 1378, but inevitably it led him into conflict with the ecclesiastical authorities — though unlike many other reformers of the time Wycliffe did die a natural death at Lutterworth. However, his enemies took out their revenge by exhuming his body, burning it, then throwing the ashes into a nearby river, on the orders of a Papal Commission in 1428.

Another early visitor to the region was the poet John Skelton (c. 1460-1529), tutor to Prince Henry (later Henry VIII), who was created 'poet-laureate' by the Universities of Oxford and Cambridge. He spent the Christmas of 1522 at Sheriff Hutton Castle, north-east of York, staying with his mother Elizabeth. (She was the daughter-in-law of the Earl of Surrey, who was given the castle after the Battle of Flodden in 1513.) Here he wrote *The Garlande of Laurell,* an allegorical poem describing how Elizabeth's ladies-in-waiting celebrate him as one of the greatest poets in the world.

Voyages overseas are very common today, and many writers publish accounts of their travels, but this was not the case when Sir Thomas Herbert (1606-1682) wrote of his expeditions. His birthplace is now a shop very near Lady Peckett's Yard along the Pavement (it has been business premises for many years), and a tablet outside a house in High Petergate commemorates the fact that he died there. His father was a prosperous merchant, but after leaving Oxford University, Thomas decided he wanted to see something of the lesser-known lands of his day. Eventually he set out on his travels, and later he recorded his impressions in books, including *Some Years Travel in Divers Parts of Asia and Africa.* In 1658 his *New and Complete Collection of Voyages and Travels* was so highly regarded it was translated into Dutch.

Not all this famous York citizen's time was spent abroad, however. During the Civil War (1642-47) he believed in the Parliamentary ideals, but in 1647 he was appointed groom of the bedchamber to attend Charles I during his imprisonment. (Charles had given himself up to the Scots, who had handed him over to the English Parliament.) Two years of imprisonment around the country followed for the unfortunate monarch. Herbert attended Charles at his execution on the 30 January 1649 at Whitehall, and as they were crossing St James' Park the king handed his testament to Herbert as a parting gift. Later he is reputed to have acquired the king's black velvet cloak which he wore on that January day. So impressed was Thomas Herbert by Charles I's dignity and conduct during his last two years of life that he wrote a book about it entitled *Threnodia Carolina*. It was published in 1678, eighteen years after Charles II had been restored to the English throne, and the new king created Herbert a baronet.

It is useless to look anywhere in York for a tablet relating to another merchant's son reputed to have been born in the city. His name is Robinson Crusoe — the fictitious hero of what is often regarded as the first English novel and one of the cornerstones of world fiction.

Daniel Defoe (1660-1731) was born in London, where his father was a tallow-chandler who spelt his name De Foe (Daniel changed his name to Defoe in 1695). At first Daniel was a haberdasher, but when his business failed in 1692 he tried again as a tile-maker, again with little success. Various occupations followed, and at one time he was employed as a secret agent travelling round the country gathering political information for the Government. In 1703 he was imprisoned for six months for writing *The Shortest Way With Dissenters* (1702), a notorious pamphlet dealing ironically with the suppression of dissent. After his release he started a periodical, *The Review,* which appeared three times a week until 1713. His first novels can be classed as a kind of early science fiction, for in 1705 was published his *A Journey to the World of the Moon,* followed by *A Letter to the Man in the Moon.*

In 1719 Defoe's industry and patience were rewarded — *Robinson Crusoe* was published. (It is interesting to note that Defoe was then almost sixty years old, which was relatively a much greater age than today.) Its author eventually became well-known, though at first his name was not mentioned on the title-page, adding to the impression that this was a true and not a fictional account. An Alexander Selkirk had experienced similar adventures in real life in 1704, and naturally many early readers believed that there had been such a man as Robinson Crusoe.

The novel's full title is *The Life and Strange and Surprising Adventures of Robinson Crusoe of York, Mariner on the Coast of America Near the Mouth of the Great River Oroonoque — Written by Himself.* The novel begins:

'I was born in the year 1632 in the city of York of a good family though not of that county, my father being a foreigner of Bremen who settled first at Hull. He got a good estate of Merchandise and leaving off his trade lived afterwards at York...'

As the novel unfolds, we learn that Crusoe was about eighteen years old when he pleaded with his parents to be allowed to go to sea, but was refused permission. One day when visiting Hull he saw a vessel almost ready to depart to London and impulsively joined the crew — his adventures had begun! (In 1973 a large bronze plaque was fixed in Queen's Gardens, Hull, to remind visitors that Crusoe had sailed from the port.)

Defoe wrote other novels, many of which read like highly romanticised biographies. He had advanced views on many aspects of life that are now taken for granted and, for example, often protested against the lack of education and training of the poor. In his preface to *Colonel Jack* (1722) he comments:

'Here is room for just and copious observations on the blessings and advantages of a sober and well-governed education, and the ruin of so many thousands of all ranks in this nation for the want of it; here also we may see how much public schools and charities might be improved, to prevent the destruction of so many unhappy children...'

The range of Defoe's writing was immense, and Alexander Pope, the eighteenth century poet and essayist, maintained Defoe wrote 'a vast many things and none bad — there is something good in all he has written'.

One of his most enduring works is his *Tour Through the Whole Island of Great Britain* (three volumes 1724-6; four volume edition 1748). It gives modern readers some idea of what various parts of the country were like in his day, and it is enlightening to compare towns and cities, and their famous buildings and industries, on a 'then-and-now' theme. His impressions are still valued by modern topographical writers and historians. Defoe visited all three ridings (his views will also occur again in appropriate parts of this book) and his Yorkshire tour ended in the capital city itself:

'We are now entering the great city of York, the Eboracum of the Romans and of such account in their time that no less than three Military Ways passed through it…In our approach to it we discovered many visible marks of Antiquity.'

He continued to suggest that any traveller interested in 'Antiquities and Curiosities' should 'make some stay in York, there being a very great variety of each to detain and amuse him'.

The Romans and their influence and the Minster appear to have been what impressed him most on his visit to the city. He compared the Minster with Lincoln Cathedral, and immediately after this section his enquiring mind prompts him to supply a comprehensive table of dates, sizes and other information about Britain's most important cathedrals and churches.

Another energetic traveller of the seventeenth and eighteenth centuries was Celia Fiennes (1662-1741), who between 1685 and 1703 visited every county in England. She was a forthright personality with quite definite opinions about the places she saw, and no record of Yorkshire's 'literary landscape' — how it would have looked to the writers of the time — would be complete without some record of her views.

In 1697 her journey north was by way of Doncaster and Tadcaster. She described Tadcaster as 'a very good little town for travellers, mostly Inns and little tradesmen's houses'; she then went on to York which she wrote of as 'standing high', though she thought it had a 'meane appearance' considering it was the See of the Archbishop of York:

'The Streets are narrow and not of any length; save one which you enter of from the bridge, that is over the Ouse, which looks like a fine river when full after much raine.'

Like many a visitor to York she stayed in an inn, though it was not quite to her liking:

'…We eat very good Cod fish and Salmon and that at a pretty cheap rate, tho' we were not in the best inn for the Angel is the best, in Coney Street.'

She goes on to describe the Pavement 'which is esteem'd the chief part of the town' and admires the many churches, especially the Minster, 'a noble building, in view at least thirty miles before you come to it...' Celia was not content merely to admire the Minster from ground level, so she climbed the Minster Tower, but the view from the top made her decide that:

'...you see all over the town that looks as a building too much clustered together, the Streets being so narrow, some were pretty long.'

She was impressed, however, with the size of the town, the buildings' windows and also the broad aisles — 'the people of fashion use them to walk in'. One thing that especially interested her was 'a mint for coyning the old money, and plate into new mill'd money'. She saw something of the work in the mint but not the actual milling, 'which art they are severe to keep private'.

On the whole Celia gave a remarkable account of her explorations in York before setting off once more on her travels to Knaresborough, one which is well worth reading in its entirety. She is another of the visitors to Yorkshire who cannot be confined to one area but keeps appearing in different parts of the county.

Probably the area's most famous literary son is an author who was not even born in this country. Lawrence Sterne (1713-1768) — whose novel, *The Life and Opinions of Tristram Shandy, Gentleman,* caused such a stir in the literary circles of the day — was born on the 24th November at Clonmel in Tipperary, Ireland. His father was serving in the army and was posted to Dunkirk, so the young Sterne was sent to live with his mother's family at Elvington just east of York, then part of the East Riding. His great-grandfather on his father's side, Richard Sterne, had been Archbishop of York from 1664 to 1683, living at Bishopthorpe Palace bordering the River Ouse a few miles from the city.

The family were noted for being members of the clergy, but though Sterne served as the incumbent of three Yorkshire parishes, it was his first novel that brought him fame. The manuscript of the first two volumes was refused in 1759 by a London publisher who would not risk his money on the strange tale of Tristram Shandy. The indefatigable Sterne paid for publication by John Hinxman, a York printer. Copies were sent to London and proved so popular that the book secured a contract from the printer-publisher who had formerly rejected it. Thus Sterne began to reap the benefits of the strange 'biography' which was completed many years later at Coxwold.

Sterne's Yorkshire links are easy enough to follow from Elvington; then to Halifax where he attended Hipperholme Grammar School before going on to Cambridge University; and then back to Yorkshire to serve in the parishes of Sutton-on-the-Forest, south-east of Thirsk, in 1738 (to which was added the parish of Stillington in 1744); and finally Coxwold, north of York.

Closely linked with York during his adult life, he lived in various dwellings, though most of them have now disappeared. One such house was in Little Alice Lane near the Minster where he courted Elizabeth Lumley, and whom he married in the Minster on the 30th March 1741. Her home is believed to have been almost opposite the fifteenth century St William's College which Sterne would have been very familiar with, though not in its present guise. St William's, named after a famous archbishop buried in the Minster's crypt, has been the home of chantry priests, a royal mint in Charles I's time, and in the mid-nineteenth century small apartments for poor people. It is now administered as a trust by the Dean and Chapter of the Minster.

This ancient building owes much to the work of Mr F Green who bought it and employed Mr Moore Temple, an eminent architect, to restore it to some of its former glory before selling it to the church authorities. Previously in 1897 he had bought the nearby Treasurer's House and lived there until 1930 when he presented it to the National Trust. Apart from its own interest, this wonderful old residence has a link with Sterne as his uncle Jacques lived in the Treasurer's House for fifteen years before selling it to Dr Toplass, an ecclesiastical lawyer portrayed in Sterne's tale *The History of a Good Warm Watch Coat* (published in 1759 as *A Political Romance*). The author had frequently written political pamphlets for his uncle Jacques before they had a violent quarrel, and his *Political Romance* was deemed so satirical that it was burned by the authorities.

Sterne's duties sometimes took him to preach at the Minster and nearby St Michael-le-Belfry Church where Guy Fawkes had been baptised. On one occasion there (rather surprisingly in view of the church's most notorious baptism) he took as his text 'Kindness the friendly softness'.

Though there are a great many differences between the fabric of York in Sterne's time and that of today, there are still many sites the literary explorer can visit which are common to both ages. It is fascinating to examine how York changed even within Sterne's lifetime, and how it compares with the city nowadays. At the time of his marriage in the Minster in 1741, the surrounding area was very different to that of today. However the house occupied by a Dr J Burton, Sterne's model for Dr Slop, the incompetent physician in *Tristram Shandy,* still exists in spacious Duncombe Place near the Minster.

Much important building work was taking place in York which Sterne would have seen in progress. The Mansion House had been built in 1725-6, and four years later saw the building of Lord Burlington's Assembly Rooms. Before 1754 what is now St Helen's Square near the Mansion House was part of the graveyard of nearby St Helen's Church. (This church, dedicated to Constantine the Great's mother, still exists as a place of worship.) Sterne would note later changes when he visited York from both Sutton and Coxwold. Fairfax House, Castlegate, near what is now the Castle Museum, was completed in 1762 as the York home of Viscount Fairfax of Emley, Ireland, the last of his line — though not to be confused with Sir Thomas Fairfax of Nun Appleton whom we shall meet in the next chapter. By the mid-twentieth century Fairfax House was much neglected, and so it was restored by the York Civic Trust at a cost of £750,000 and opened to the public in 1984.

As was customary — especially with clergy attached to the Minster — Sterne had a town house. On two occasions at least this was in mediaeval Stonegate, the thoroughfare from Minster Gate to St Helen's Square. Along here an old shop displaying the date 1683 and a sign of the Bible can still be seen. This was once owned by Hildyard,

An eighteenth century view of the Assembly Rooms, built by
Lord Burlington.

Laurence Sterne.

Shandy Hall.

The dining room at Shandy Hall. It has been reconstructed to show how it was in Sterne's time.

printer, publisher and the most fashionable bookseller in York, who is reputed to have stocked over 30,000 books in many foreign languages. After his death, John Hinxman took over the business and it was he who first published and issued *Tristram Shandy.*

The social life of York was also very important to its inhabitants, and such moot points as whether Dr Slop was really based on Dr Burton would be aired in the coffee houses. Sterne was also a coffee house frequenter, but his favourite, Sunton's in Coney Street, has since disappeared. Another haunt of his, the George Inn, also in Coney Street, has now been business premises for many years.

Leaving York for Coxwold, as Sterne did in 1760 to spend his last eight years as its vicar, even more interesting associations can be explored. Here his happiest days were spent in the old hall he named Shandy Hall after the family he created, and it has remained Shandy Hall ever since he moved in. However when he became Vicar of Coxwold there was no official clergyman's house, so this mid-fifteenth century timber-framed hall-house not far from the church was acquired. (It was originally built as a priest's house.) Several alterations have changed some parts of the building over the centuries, but essentially it remains as he would have known it. Indeed the sash windows may have been one of the improvements he carried out during his time here. A little room by the front door was lined books and used as a study, and it was here that Sterne wrote further volumes of *Tristram Shandy* (volumes two to six published 1761; volumes seven and eight, 1765; volume nine, 1767); *A Sentimental Journey Through France and Italy* (1768), which resulted from his travels between 1762 and 1764 to try and cure his failing health; and *Journal to Eliza,* written in 1767.

He maintained:

'I am as happy as a Prince at Coxwold and I wish you could see in how private a manner I live. 'Tis a land of plenty, I sit down alone to venison, fish and wild fowl, or a couple of fowls or duck with curds and strawberries and cream and all the plenty which a rich valley under the Hambleton Hills can provide.

I am in high spirits and care never enters this cottage.'

One of his favourite outings was to nearby Byland Abbey, which he described:

'...When I go to visit my ruin, I give this title to an afternoon's pilgrimage I frequently make, to the ruins of a Benedictine monastery about a mile and a half from my cottage.

These remains are situated on the bank of a clear gliding stream on the opposite side whereof rises a bald ridge of hills, thick with woods...

To this place after my coffee, unless prevented by inclement skies I guide my daily steps.'

Sterne's life here was cut short during a visit to his London publisher in 1768, and he died of pleurisy on the 18th March. Like his writings, even his burial in London followed no orthodox pattern, and it is believed that his body was stolen by resurrectionists who later replaced it after it was recognised at an anatomy lecture. When that particular graveyard was cleared for building development in the late 1960's, the Laurence Sterne Trust had the author's body exhumed and re-interred in Coxwold churchyard near the church door.

Lovers of this eighteenth century clergyman's work owe a tremendous debt to the trust, for up to fifteen years ago visitors to Coxwold could only see the exterior of Shandy Hall. Now thousands of visitors from all over the world make a special pilgrimage to beautiful Coxwold just to call at the mediaeval house where Sterne once lived.

In 1963 when the scholar Kenneth Monkman and his wife Julia visited Coxwold they were appalled at the neglected state of Shandy Hall, and decided that something must be done to save this literary treasure, not only for Britain, but also for the rest of the world. Before long their keen interest, insight and enthusiasm inspired other scholars and well-known personalities to join the campaign. The Laurence Sterne Trust was set up in 1968 with Kenneth Monkman as honorary secretary. An appeal was launched to raise £25,000 to buy the freehold of the cottage to mark the bicentenary of Sterne's death, and to restore what has been described as 'the earliest, most unspoilt survival of a famous novelist's home in Britain'.

Many eminent people became members of the trust, including the

Ryedale-born poet and art critic, Sir Herbert Read; William Rees-Mogg, then editor of *The Times* (Sir William, as he now is, still serves on the trust); Professor L P Curtis of the department of history, Yale University; Canon R Cant, chancellor and librarian of York Minster; and Professor J P Brockbank, head of the department of English at the University of York.

Prior to the museum's opening Kenneth Monkman told the writer:

'We hope to put on display that which will catch the interest of those who know nothing of Sterne, and will fascinate those who know a great deal.'

That aim has surely been achieved. The majority of visitors are keenly interested in the book-lined study where Sterne did much of his writing. Many of the books in this little study are first or rare editions of Sterne's books, comprising 250 volumes and representing the most comprehensive collection of his works anywhere in the world. There are also other valuable volumes and documents, such as letters, autographed tithe accounts and newspapers such as the *York Gazetteer* for which Sterne wrote. All these are from Kenneth Monkman's own vast collection, which he began over fifty years ago, and have been on loan to the trust ever since the museum was opened by Frank Muir in 1973. The fine furniture, paintings and other items that convey the atmosphere of the gracious lifestyle Sterne enjoyed are also on loan from the Monkman family.

Shandy Hall's lovely eighteenth century walled gardens also delight many people, including the new one-acre wild garden. These are specially opened on certain summer Sundays as part of the National Garden Scheme for Yorkshire, and have been recreated by keen gardener Julia Monkman, now the honorary curator and honorary secretary of the trust.

Recently the trust has launched an appeal, again backed by many eminent figures and university authorities, both to purchase the unique Monkman collection and secure the future of Shandy Hall. Plans include transforming the granary into accommodation for research students, and the University of York intends to create two fellowships in Sterne studies. It is also planned to engage a full-time curator and extend the opening times so that an increased number of tourists and local visitors alike can explore the beautiful Shandy Hall, and learn more about the man about whom J B Priestley said:

'Modern literature begins with Sterne. He seems to jump clean out of the ponderous eighteenth century, testing our patience, into our own time, impatient of inessentials.'

York can also lay claim to its own Poet Laureate, though one who perhaps did not deserve the position as much as others. Laurence Eusden (1688-1730) was born at Spofforth near Harrogate, and educated at St Peter's School, which is now part of Clifton. He was rather unjustly made Poet Laureate in 1718 after he wrote highly complimentary verses for the marriage of the Duke of Newcastle, who then obtained the position for him. He wrote little of worth, and his dissolute habits were satirised by Alexander Pope, among others.

It is likely that Eusden's exploits and lack of talent would have incurred the wrath of another eighteenth century writer who visited York who often used his wit to devastating effect, though luckily for Eusden he was only a young boy while he was Poet Laureate. Dr Samuel Johnson (1709-1784) was born in Lichfield, Staffordshire, and was from an early age a great reader, enjoying nothing more than browsing along his father's bookshop shelves. His life is a fascinating one because he took such an interest in what was happening around him in the world. James Boswell's *Life of Johnson* (1791) provides some amusing and illuminating glimpses of the 'great Doctor' and the times in which he lived.

At first Johnson was a teacher, but in 1737 he decided to move to London accompanied by David Garrick, who later became a famous actor. (At the time of their arrival in the capital they are reputed to have possessed only fivepence between them.) Johnson set about earning his living by writing essays and editing publications, but it was the compiling of his *Lexicography* (dictionary) that made him famous. He also gained quite a reputation as a man with forthright opinions on many subjects. He was not merely a 'literary lion', however, but a man of genuine compassion and interest in his fellow human beings — though perhaps sometimes rather pompous in the way he expressed that interest.

He visited York in 1773 on his way to Scotland with Boswell, and called in at the Minster, especially admiring the fine chapter house. (Like other tourists of his day he had to be content to see St Mary's Abbey ruins from a distance.) Then he ambled along to the Debtor's Prison, which was then housed in the elegant building now part of the Castle Museum. Here he was impressed to learn that the head jailor, William Clayton, had once been imprisoned for debt, but had so proved his worth that the governor had first made him jailor and subsequently head jailor. He was also much impressed with the buildings that have now been transformed into the world-famous museum founded by Dr John Kirk, its first curator. It was his vast collection of bygones that formed the nucleus of the museum when it first opened in 1938.

Samuel Taylor Coleridge (1772-1834) visited York in 1799 and it is likely that, as did so many eighteenth century visitors to the city, he went down to the river to see the busy staithes and the shipping. A riverside walk had been specially created not far from Clifford's Tower and the Debtor's Prison.

No doubt Percy Bysshe Shelley (1792-1822) had more pressing concerns on his visit in late 1811 than a walk down the banks of the Ouse or to the Minster. First he had been expelled from Oxford in March of that year for writing the pamphlet *The Necessity of Atheism;* then he entered into a disastrous relationship with Harriet Westbrook, the sixteen year old daughter of a London coffee-house owner, with whom he ran away and married in Edinburgh in August 1811. (The marriage lasted only three years, and Harriet committed suicide in 1816.) On the return journey they stayed in York and seemed to do nothing but complain about the accommodation — they regarded the town as being 'dingy'. At first they stayed with two elderly milliners, the Misses Dancer, near the Black Swan on Coney Street (now gone); then they moved to Miss Strickland's in Blake Street. Not even the presence of his friend Thomas Jefferson Hogg — who had also been sent down from Oxford with him and lived at 20 Coney Street — pleased the poet. During his brief stay here, Shelley tried to appease his father about his sudden marriage. He is also reputed to have written a little of his poem *Queen Mab* during his time in York.

When H V Morton, researching for his book *The Call of England* (1928), visited York Castle, it was as a special favour that he was shown Dick Turpin's cell where the highwayman had spent his last few weeks before his execution in 1739. (Modern visitors can now enjoy the visit as part of the tour of the museum.) Even so, it was 'Swift John' Nevison, another daring robber, who really made the famous ride, not Turpin. However, the novelist Harrison Ainsworth (1805-1882) did much to promote the legend of Dick Turpin when he gave the wrong highwayman the credit in his highly romanticised *Rookwood* (1834). Ainsworth left an account of twenty four hours of continuous work:

'I began in the morning and wrote all day and as the night wore on my subject had completely mastered me, and I had no power to leave Turpin on the high road. I was swept away by the curious excitement and novelty of the situation and being personally a good horseman and passionately fond of horses — I was thoroughly at home with my work, and galloped on with my pet highwayman merrily enough.'

Rookwood was his most famous work, though he wrote other full-blooded historical novels concerning the exploits of villains that especially grip the imagination of children. Apart from novels, Ainsworth also edited and owned the *New Monthly Magazine,* and is reputed to have been a model editor — prompt in payment, courteous and kind. He even went so far as to advise on other markets when a submission did not suit his own magazine.

During its long history many well-known people have attended the enthronement of successive Archbishops of York in the Minster. One of these was Ralph Waldo Emerson (1803-1882) who attended such a service in 1848. This American author is now best-remembered for his *Essays,* the first series published in 1841 and the second series three years later.

When Emerson was first invited to England on a lecture tour between 1848 and 1849 he said:

'I feel no call to make a visit of literary propagandum in England

— in no one city, except perhaps in London, could I find any numerous company to whom my name is favourably known.'

He was wrong, however, as he discovered on his visit, and one outcome of his tour was a book entitled *English Traits* (1865). His invitation was mainly given by the Mechanics' Institutes of Lancashire and Yorkshire. No literary study, especially in Yorkshire, is complete without mention of such institutes. Most famous men of the nineteenth century, including Ruskin and Dickens, lectured at the various branches. They were the equivalent of the working man's extra-mural classes in the days when manual workers and tradesmen had little hope of attending college or university. In their scant leisure time they were encouraged to join the Mechanics' Institutes and hear informative lectures on literature, science and other subjects, and borrow books from the library. Many of the Victorian buildings in the north were specially built for this purpose and carry the name engraved on the front.

When Emerson visited the Minster there was no voluntary guide to provide him with information as there are now. Indeed nobody seems to have told him the erroneous story of the Five Sisters Window which Charles Dickens heard, and used in *Nicholas Nickleby*.

As the coach with Nicholas Nickleby, Mr Squeers and the six new pupils journeyed north, it overturned. Nobody was injured, but to pass the time until another coach arrived, two gentlemen each offered to tell a story. A grey-haired gentleman, who had proved himself a talkative person even before the accident, began with the story of the Five Sisters Window in York Minster. Hundreds of years ago, five young and very lovely girls were in the care of St Mary's Abbey. One of the monks tried again and again to persuade them to become nuns, but they would not entertain the idea. He was particularly annoyed to see them wasting their time embroidering a large tapestry divided into five panels. One day the eldest sister told him that the tapestry had been designed by their mother who was now dead. She had advised them to complete it and then at some future date, when they might be unhappy, the tapestry would bring back memories of more joyful times.

Time passed. The sisters married and were widowed. Alice, the youngest and most beautiful, had died. They returned to the abbey and the monk saw them in their black robes. Again he advised them to destroy the completed tapestry and enter a convent — it was not too late to do so. Instead of following his advice they decided that the tapestry should be the basis of a window in the Minster. The eldest sister engaged skilled artists and craftsmen from abroad who used the tapestry's design to complete a lovely window.

'There it is to this day', Dickens' narrator pointed out.

Whatever opinon readers may have of Dickens' story, there is no doubt about the beauty of the window. In his novel *The Houses Inbetween* (1951), Howard Spring gives a description of the re-dedication of this window in the 1920's. It had been restored after World War I in memory of the women of the Empire who lost their lives in that conflict. The unveiling was carried out by the then Duchess of York, now Queen Elizabeth the Queen Mother. (Although not a Yorkshireman, Howard Spring is an author connected with the region who is most frequently 'met' in the West Riding.)

Not all visitors have called in at the Minster. In October 1820 the critic and historian Thomas Carlyle (1795-1881) visited the city in the hope of being engaged as a travelling tutor to a family in the area. This was on the recommendation of his friend Thomas Allen, the apothecary of York County Asylum. The job sounded inviting enough — £150 a year and 'all found'. Yet Carlyle, after weighing up the pros and cons, decided against it. His disappointment at not obtaining a really congenial position may have caused him to take a dislike to York, though he considered Yorkshire 'a most rich and picturesque county'.

Like Laurence Sterne, another clergyman-writer who came to live in Yorkshire was Essex-born Sydney Smith, though unlike Sterne the very idea of coming north at first horrified him. Known as the 'Smith of Smiths', in 1802 he co-founded the influential *Edinburgh Review* — some of whose reviews made authors almost sick with apprehension — and he edited three issues and contributed to others. Most of his work only interests scholars today, but his personality will still appeal

Sydney Smith.

The river walk in the eighteenth century. 'This Pleasant Walk is near a mile in length, but for the Advantage of seeing the fine Bridge and Cathedral &c This view was taken from near the Centre.' One can see the bridge and beyond it the Minster and a section of what is now the Castle Museum.

A View of Castle Howard by Henrick de Cort, c.1800. This elegant eighteenth century mansion was visited by Sydney Smith, Dickens and Sir John Betjeman.

to anyone fascinated with unusual characters. Writing to Lady Georgina Morpeth he set down some of his rules of life:

'Take short views of life, not farther than dinner or tea. Don't expect too much of life, a sorry business at the best. Don't be too severe on yourself, or underrate yourself, but do yourself justice.'

'Whatever you are from nature keep to it, never desert your own line of talent. Be what nature intended you for, and you will succeed, be anything else and you will be ten thousand times worse than nothing.'

He had been seeking a regular income in a non-residential parish for some time before he was appointed rector of Foston-le-Clay, north-east of York. At that time it was quite usual for clergymen to be incumbents of parishes to which they never went, and usually the work in the parish concerned would be done by poorly-paid clergy. (Anthony Trollope wrote of this practise in his novel *Barchester Towers.*) When a clergyman was needed for Foston, Lady Holland persuaded Thomas Erskine, the Lord Chancellor in the Ministry of All Talents, to appoint Smith to this Chancery living in 1806. He gratefully accepted, and Erskine replied to him on the 6th October 1806:

'I should be guilty of insincerity, and be taking a merit with you, which I have no claim to, if I were not to say that I should have given the living to the nominee of Lord and Lady Holland without any personal consideration...'

He went on to add that he regarded himself fortunate that they had selected someone like Smith.

After his appointment as Rector of Foston with Thornton-le-Clay, Smith continued to live in the south while a clergyman from York took the services. The Clergy Residency Act of 1803 was not being strictly enforced by Archbishop Markham of York, but after his death and the appointment of Archbishop Harcourt, Smith decided in 1808 to take up residence in his parish. There was no parsonage, so he rented a house at Heslington (now part of York University) for himself, his wife and his children.

In 1814 Smith decided that the time had come for Foston to have a rectory. He knew exactly what kind of house he needed, and what is more he persuaded the rather phlegmatic ecclesiastical authorities to grant him a loan to build the rectory. This came mainly from Queen Anne's Bounty (the forerunner of the much-altered modern Church Commissioners) and was for the sum of £1,600 to be repaid at £130 per year. As the architect's plans did not please the Rev Sydney and Mrs Smith they designed their own ideal home which cost in the region of £4,000 — Smith having to supply the balance himself. The Old Rectory was situated between Foston and Thornton-le-Clay. In 1962 a fire unfortunately destroyed the original house, but it was rebuilt as much like Smith's Old Rectory as possible. It can be visited by those who wish to gain some impression of the home life of this clergyman and wit.

Being unable to make his £600 a year stipend plus income from writing cover all his expenses, he turned serious attention to farming. Like most country parishes he owned glebe land — a portion of land for the incumbent's use, whether he farmed it himself or let it to a neighbour. Nor did agricultural pursuits occupy all Smith's time, as he tried to cure his parishioners' bodies as well as their souls — probably more so. Before long this clergyman-author-farmer-apothecary was affectionately regarded by his new congregation, though when he had first arrived in the area he had humourously written:

'The people here are converted to the Christian faith, wear clothes and understand the principles of truck and barter. Justice can generally be obtained by applying to the Sheik or Lord Mayor of York and the stories of cannibalism are utterly unfounded.'

He was obviously enjoying his life here as best he could, for when Lady Holland once wrote sympathetically to him because of his dull life, he replied:

'...if life is the choice, then it is common-sense to amuse yourself with the best you can find where you happen to be placed.'

He continued that although he was not living as he would have chosen, he was determined not to be unhappy.

Certainly if a busy life ensures happiness, Smith must have been supremely happy. Even granted that an early nineteenth century day would last much longer than in modern times, his were full of work and study. Not content with a merely rural life, he was also an important cleric in York, preaching the assize sermon and carrying out other duties.

Anyone seeking the landscape Smith knew should visit the Old Rectory and also the small — though altered — church of All Saints, Foston. It contains a memorial in his honour, with a profile of him and the tribute:

'He was a faithful friend and counsellor, a seeker of peace and a wit who used his power to delight and not to wound.'

He moved from Foston to the West Country in 1828, and was later appointed a canon of St Paul's Cathedral in 1831. But while living in Yorkshire he loved to visit his friends to enjoy their hospitality and discuss books with them. One of his favourite places was Hunmanby Vicarage, just inland from the coast below Filey. Here Smith delighted in visiting the Rev Francis Wrangham, Vicar of Hunmanby from 1795 to 1840. He liked nothing better than visiting his friend and borrowing some of his fine volumes. Born at Raisthorpe near Malton, the son of a farmer, Wrangham was a wealthy clergyman whose love of reading prompted him to found a local library for his parishioners. Book buying must have been Wrangham's main hobby, for it is told how he visited many parts of the country buying valuable collections, and would not quibble at the price if he saw a book he desired. Indeed in 1803 he had built a new wing to the vicarage to house all his books. Eventually the Rev F Wrangham became Archdeacon of Cleveland and the East Riding before moving to Chester, where he died in 1842 a few years before his old friend.

Modern visitors retracing Sydney Smith's literary landscape in the Foston area should enjoy an outing to one of Smith's favourite mansions nearby: magnificent Castle Howard, set in vast parklands, was designed by the architect and playwright Sir John Vanburgh in the early eighteenth century. Smith often stayed there and received many kindnesses from Lord and Lady Carlisle, who had first visited the Old Rectory in 1815.

Smith is not the only famous writer to have links with Castle Howard. The seventh Earl of Carlisle often corresponded with Charles Dickens, who was a frequent visitor to his friend Charles Smithson of Easthorpe Hall, Malton. In the summer of 1843 Dickens and his wife spent a few weeks with Mr Smithson, and visited Castle Howard, Old Malton Abbey Church and Kirkham Abbey ruins. Other writers who had connections with Castle Howard's former owners, the ninth Earl and Countess, were Alfred Lord Tennyson, Robert Browning and William Morris. In more recent times Sir John Betjeman wrote about the stately home in a TV film *Bird's Eye View*, and his lines were published in *The Listener* of the 2nd June 1977. Even if the general public are not familiar with it through its literary connections, they will surely recognise Castle Howard when they realise that it featured in the TV version of Evelyn Waugh's novel *Brideshead Revisited.*

We can visualise the city of York in the nineteenth century with the observations of another famous literary figure, this time from overseas. The American novelist Nathaniel Hawthorne (1804-1864) was another traveller who, as well as being one of the fathers of American fiction, also recorded his journeys for posterity. Of him the Yorkshire-born poet and critic Sir Herbert Read wrote that 'In any general view of the whole of American literature, the first peak we discern is Hawthorne', and called him 'one of the world's great imaginative writers'.

It was quite usual for American authors during the last century to visit or live in Europe for a time, and then write up their impressions for publication back home. Nathaniel Hawthorne was such a writer and his *Our Old Home* was published in 1863 (a good edition of this work is the one of 1883, *Our Old Home and English Notebooks).*

Hawthorne always had a discerning eye for architecture, climate and amusing characters, and was by no means reticent when it came to penning genuine reactions to these. His visits in Yorkshire were to places such as Skipton and Bolton Abbey (to which he gives its correct name of Bolton Priory), and his comments on these places will be noted in the appropriate chapter.

Born in Salem, Massachusetts, he began to write stories when quite young and decided from an early age that he would be an author. The first part of his early working life was spent in authorship, and many of the tales he wrote were based on his own New England region. His first novel, *Fanshawe* (1828), was published at his own expense. Then, like many other writers both before and since, he took another job for financial reasons in the Boston Custom House, though eventually reverted to full-time writing. In spite of the break in his employment with the Custom House, it did eventually lead to his appointment as American consul in Liverpool from 1853 to 1857. By the time he arrived in this country, Hawthorne was the successful author of *The Scarlet Letter* (1850), *The House of the Seven Gables* (1851) and other novels; his *Tanglewood Tales,* based on ancient legends for children, was published in 1853.

Although Hawthorne did not set any of his books in Britain, he did write part of one novel in Redcar. After a two year stay in Europe where his daughter Una had been taken very ill at Rome, he and his family stayed for a short time at Whitby and then moved to Redcar. He and his wife had chosen this quiet seaside town because it was not so expensive as Whitby, though Whitby was not so expensive as Scarborough — or so Mrs Hawthorne reported to her sister. The publishing firm of Smith Elder had offered Hawthorne £600 for the British rights of his new novel, so each day he worked from nine o'clock in the morning until three in the afternoon in a house only twenty yards from 'the German Ocean', at 120 High Street. The novel was entitled *Transformation: The Romance of Monte Beni* (1860) for the English edition and *The Marble Faun: A Romance of Mount Beni* in America.

When living in Liverpool, Southport and Birkenhead, Hawthorne enjoyed nothing better than taking his wife, son Julian and little Una exploring. He did not regard himself as a good sightseer, 'at least I soon get satisfied with looking at set sights and wish to go on to the next', he wrote. Best of all he loved to wander around in search of his own literary and historical discoveries — a method he heartily recommended.

His first visit to York was in 1856 when returning from Scotland by train:

'It was about 11 o'clock when I beheld York Cathedral above the old city which stands on the River Ouse separated by it from the railway station [this was York's first railway station, not the present one which was built in 1877], but communicating by a Ferry (or two) and a bridge, I wandered forth and found my way over the latter into the ancient and irregular streets of York'.

It impressed him as 'a quaint old place and what looked most modern is probably something old hiding itself behind a new front as elsewhere in England'. Although he admired old churches, his first verdict on the Minster was that 'I doubt whether a cathedral is a sort of edifice suited to the English climate'. (Was he thinking of long services in icy churches?)

Up and down the narrow streets he strolled, but could not discover his way back to the railway station until a York gentleman took him around the walls and eventually to the Ouse ferry. The cheap fare of a half-penny and the fact that the ferryman refused a tip struck him as 'wonderful'.

On a subsequent visit in April 1857 he, his wife and Julian found York even more pleasant. They had been spending a few days at Skipton and Wharfedale, and travelled to York by train from Leeds. The inn they stayed at was the Black Swan on Coney Street, of which Hawthorne wrote:

'It is a very ancient hotel for in the coffee-house I saw on the wall an old poster announcing that a stage-coach would leave the Black Swan in York in four days and dated 1706. It is a very good hotel.'

Unfortunately the inn no longer exists, being swept away by developments years ago.

He relates how he and his family went out before tea 'to get a glimpse of the cathedral, which impressed me more grandly than when I first saw it a year ago'. They then explored 'a narrow crooked street, very old and very shabby, but with an antique house — portal arch — paved quadrangle'. Later they returned again to look at 'the College', as St William's College was called, and Hawthorne stated

Inside of the City Walls, 1807.

The Black Swan on Coney Street. From *The Old Coaching Days in Yorkshire*
(1889) by Tom Bradley.

A 1760 view of the grandstand at Knavesmire Racecourse, York.

it 'was let in rooms and small tenements to poor people'. As it was Easter Sunday, the Hawthornes attended service at the Minster. Although his impression of the building was that it was 'very stately and very beautiful — and doubtless would be very satisfactory could I only know it long and well enough', he did not care for the service. He longed for a shorter service and a much longer sermon — as a New Englander, Hawthorne enjoyed sermons of at least an hour and a half in duration. He did, however, comment:

'I thank God that I saw the Cathedral again and I thank Him that He inspired the builders to make it and that mankind has so long enjoyed it.'

One thing that greatly disappointed Julian and himself was their inability to gain admittance to the museum gardens and inspect St Mary's Abbey ruins. Instead they had to be content merely to gaze through the iron railings.

Only a few years later another adult and child were looking round York. On the 3rd January 1863 a small Scottish boy and his nurse Cummy were in York on their way abroad. 'Lou', as Cummy called her charge Robert Louis Stevenson (1850-1894), delighted in the old city. He insisted on taking her for a midnight walk on the walls and round by the river. Such a walk (though not at midnight!) is still one of the best ways of seeing the city and its landmarks. Stevenson saw what is now one of the best-known features of York. At the time of his visit, the new Lendal Bridge, designed by Thomas Page, was almost completed and due to be opened on the 22nd January 1863. A plaque on this fine bridge states that it was a toll bridge until the end of the century, when the toll was abolished.

Stevenson always maintained that Cummy had encouraged him to become a writer by listening to his stories when he was quite small — though it was true she had often chided him for talking nonsense. His first book, *The Pentland Rising,* was published at his father's expense. He refused to enter the family's lighthouse engineering firm, though he did consent to study law at Edinburgh University for a time. He eventually found fame as the author of such books as *Treasure Island* (1883), *The Strange Case of Dr Jekyll and Mr Hyde* (1886) and *Kidnapped*

(1886), though he battled courageously with ill-health, notably tuberculosis, throughout his life.

All this was in the future, however, when he and Cummy wandered around the walls late that January night, and it was she who eventually described their visit in her journal.

Another small boy, so tiny as to be still a baby when he left York, was Wystan Hugh Auden (1907-1973). He was the son of Dr George Augustus Auden, and born at 54 Bootham. (The York Civic Trust arranged that a plaque should mark his birthplace and this was unveiled on the 11th March 1975.) Although Dr Auden had edited a book about York for the seventy-fifth meeting of the British Association in 1906, his son found even more fame. Educated at Christ Church, Oxford, he later became a teacher in both England and Scotland. Poetry was his main interest, however, and his first collection was published in 1930, entitled simply *Poems*. Two years later came the publication of *The Orators,* and from then on he was regarded as the leading English poet of his age. He also wrote for the theatre, notably *The Dog Beneath the Skin* (1935) and *The Ascent of F6* (1936), both in collaboration with Christopher Isherwood. In January 1939 Auden moved to America where he lived for many years, and in time became an American citizen. In 1956 he returned to England and became professor of poetry at Oxford, a position he held for four years. He also published books of essays, one of his last being *The Dyers Hand and Other Essays* (1963).

Although none of his work had much connection with his native city, W H Auden did encourage his readers in an attitude that most inhabitants of York would approve — the ability to read carefully what he wrote and through his work develop their own sense of self-awareness.

The East Coast

In a literary survey such as this it is often possible to 'journey' through a particular region, and nowhere is this more so than the rolling Wolds and coast of the former East Riding, where it is simple to travel up the coastline and survey each town individually.

Like York with its mystery plays, the old East Riding can also lay claim to a literary tradition of hundreds of years. The town of Grimsby has a strong connection with early English literature, since its very name comes from a character in a thirteenth century verse romance. In *The Lay of Havelok the Dane* the hero flees from his homeland and is brought up in Grimsby by the fisherman Grim, who subsequently returns with Havelok to Denmark to help him reclaim his rightful kingship. The kindly fisherman also features in the port's seal.

The East Riding played an important part in English history, and this is especially so of Hull. Most important of the events centred on this fishing port is the seventeenth century Civil War between the Royalist and Parliamentary forces. Though he played no active part in these, John Evelyn (1620-1706) is of interest because of his portrayal of the region in these troubled times. Born at Wotton House in Surrey, he became one of the most eminent gentlemen of the time, and was acquainted with many important seventeenth century poets, authors and scientists. Keenly interested in gardening, history, architecture and astrology, he was a member of the Royal Society and its secretary in 1673.

He also kept a *Diary* (not discovered and published until 1818; six volume edition published 1955) which provides a fascinating picture of seventeenth century life. As he journeyed about the land, visiting famous mansions and staying in ancient towns, he noted down his impressions. These visits included many in Yorkshire, both in the south at such places as Doncaster, in the north and in the east.

Evelyn visited York in 1658, just before Charles II's restoration to the throne. His eyesight must have been remarkable, or as a scientific man he must have used some kind of an 'eyeglass', for he recorded:

'I got up to the town, whence we had a prospect towards Durham, and could see Ripon, part of Lancashire, the famous and fatal Marston Moor [where a crucial Civil War battle had been fought in 1644], the Spa of Knaresborough and all the environs of that remarkable county...'

He had previously visited Beverley on the 16th August 1654:

'We went to Beverley, a large town with two stately churches, St John's [the Minster] and St Mary's, not much inferior to the best of our cathedrals. Here a very old woman showed us the monuments and being about 100 years old, spoke the language of Queen Mary's time in which she had been born, she was the widow of a Sexton who had belonged to the church.'

There is very little chance of modern visitors being greeted by such a venerable church guide, but the two churches are still worth visiting, as is ancient Beverley itself.

At the time of John Evelyn's visit to East Yorkshire, a contemporary of his was soon to become one of Hull's most famous sons. Andrew Marvell (1621-1678), Hull's poet-patriot, was born at Winestead east of Hull where his father was rector. In 1624 the family moved to Hull where Mr Marvell became a lecturer at Holy Trinity Church and master of the Charterhouse. (Unfortunately he died by drowning in the Humber in 1641.) The young Marvell attended Hull Grammar School before going to Trinity College, Cambridge, where he gained a BA in 1639. After some years' travel abroad, he became Hull's first Member of Parliament in January 1659, a constituency he served until his death nineteen years later. While MP he kept Hull Corporation well informed as to what was happening in Richard Cromwell's new Parliament, and over 300 of his letters reporting the political events of his day are in the city's archives.

During his lifetime he was celebrated as a satirist and a defender of liberty — in 1650 he wrote what is often regarded as the greatest political poem in the English language, *An Horatian Ode Upon Cromwell's Return from Ireland* — and he was often engaged in dangerous

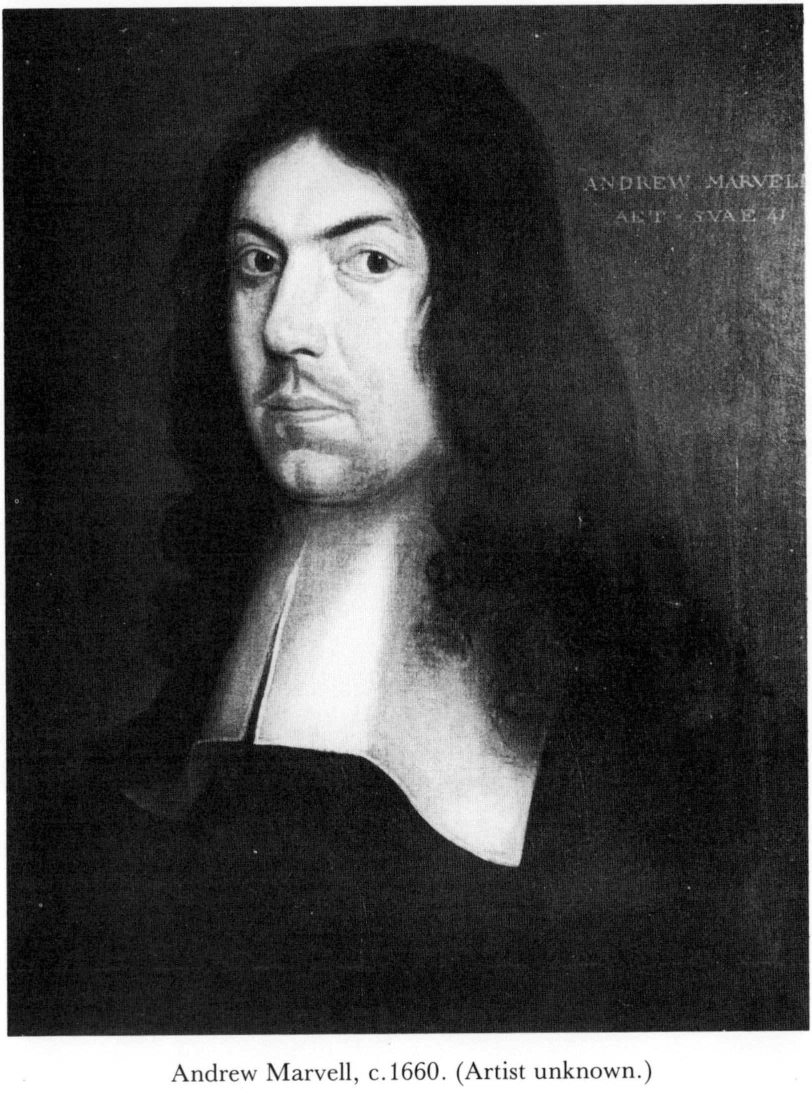

Andrew Marvell, c.1660. (Artist unknown.)

Holy Trinity Church, Hull, one of the largest parish churches in the country and an outstanding example of fourteenth century architecture. Andrew Marvell's father was rector here, as at a later date was the father of the poet and clergyman William Mason.

Nun Appleton Hall.

political business. In 1678 a reward was offered by the *London Gazette* for information about the author of the anonymous pamphlet *An Account of the Growth of Popery and Arbitrary Government in England* (1677) — which was written by Marvell.

Yet it is as lyric poet that he is remembered today, especially for the two long poems he wrote at Nun Appleton House (or Hall), near Appleton Roebuck just east of Tadcaster, home of the third Lord Fairfax (1612-1671). This famous Parliamentary general was better-known during his army career as Sir Thomas Fairfax, or 'Black Tom' on account of his complexion. He had been knighted by Charles I after the first Scottish war of his reign, but joined the Parliamentary forces during the Civil War.

Although Nun Appleton House is better connected by its location to the York area, its association with Marvell merit its inclusion in this chapter.

Nun Appleton dates from 1150, when a Cistercian monastery was founded here. After the dissolution of the monasteries in 1542, the property eventually passed to the Fairfaxes. A mansion was erected but later demolished, and its brick successor, planned and built by the first Lord Fairfax (Sir Thomas's grandfather), was the one known to Marvell. Later in 1770 the wings of this house were demolished by the then owner and the house rebuilt, with only some parts remaining of the Fairfax home. (The poet and scholar Sir Francis Hastings Doyle (1810-1888) was born here in what was his grandfather's home and described it in *Reminiscences and Opinions* (1886) as 'an ugly place', with little in common with the seventeenth century dwelling.)

Andrew Marvell became tutor to Lord and Lady Fairfax's daughter Mary (Moll to her father and Maria in Marvell's poems) either in late 1650 or early 1651. Here he enjoyed a pleasant, unde-manding existence for two years, a period of his life which has been judged as being very important to his literary career. Judging by the verse he wrote during this time, *Upon Appleton House, The Garden* and the 'Mower' series of poems, this is certainly true.

The parkland contained the remains of an old nunnery, closer to the mansion were flower gardens — which especially delighted Lord

Fairfax — and meadows stretched to the banks of the River Wharfe. Something of the beauty of the house and its surroundings can be gleaned from Marvell's poems. The fifth verse of *The Garden* reads:

> 'What wondrous life is this I lead!
> Ripe apples drop about my head;
> The luscious clusters of the vine
> Upon my mouth do crush their wine;
> The nectarine and curious peach,
> Into my hands themselves do reach;
> Stumbling on melons as I pass,
> Insnar'd with flow'rs, I fall on grass.'

And from the poem's final verse:

> 'And as it works the industrious bee
> Computes its time as well as we.
> How could such sweet and wholesome hours
> Be reckoned but with herbs and flowers.'

He also wrote *The Hill and Grove at Bill-borough* dedicated to 'My Lord Fairfax'. This nobleman had family properties at both Denton near Ilkley, and Bilbrough north of Nun Appleton:

> 'His Bishop-hill, or Denton may
> Of Bill-borough, better hold than they,
> But nature here hath been so free
> As if she said leave this to me;
> Art would more neatly have defac'd
> What she had laid so sweetly waste
> In fragrant gardens, shady woods,
> Deep meadows and transparent floods.'

Like Nun Appleton, the above-mentioned place is worth visiting for its own sake as well as for its literary associations. Lord Fairfax and his wife are buried in the chapel of the mediaeval church at Bilbrough. The church was replaced in 1873 by a larger one, but the magnificent tomb in its ancient chapel remains. In 1984 a public appeal was announced to restore the tomb of this famous Yorkshire gentleman

Hull Grammar School, attended in the seventeenth century by Andrew Marvell and at a later date by William Wilberforce.

The Fairfax tomb, containing the bodies of Sir Thomas Fairfax and his wife, in the old chapel of Bilbrough Church.

E C Booth.

who had done so much to prevent many of England's finest treasures being destroyed in the Civil War. (These included the stained glass of York Minster.) By permission of the Dean and Chapter of York, the restoration of the Fairfax tomb was carried out by the Minster's own craftsmen. On the 13th June 1986, Dr John Habgood, the Archbishop of York, preached at a thanksgiving service at Bilbrough Church in honour of the life and service of Sir Thomas Fairfax.

After he left Nun Appleton, Marvell was briefly the tutor of Oliver Cromwell's ward William Dutton, and then in 1657 was appointed secretary to his friend John Milton, who was Latin secretary to the newly-formed Council of State. When Milton was imprisoned after the Restoration, Marvell interceded on his behalf and helped obtain his release. (The second edition of Milton's *Paradise Lost* contained a commendatory poem by Marvell.) He continued to write poetry, but none as accomplished as that which he wrote in his home county. He wrote one, *To Dr Witty,* in honour of a Hull physician who had been a master at the grammar school from 1636 to 1642.

Some of his later works have curious titles which do little to indicate their true subject matter. For example, *The Last Instructions to a Painter* (1667) does not deal with artistic matters, but is a satire on courtly and parliamentary corruption. This was not published until after his death, as was *A Dialogue Between Two Horses,* first printed in *Poems on Affairs of State* (1689); this depicts an imaginary conversation between steeds being 'riden' by the statues of Charles I and Charles II. But probably his best-known lines are from *To His Coy Mistress:*

> "Had we but world enough, and time,
> This coyness, Lady, were no crime,
> We would sit down, and think which way
> To walk, and pass our long love's day,
> Thou by the Indian Gange's side
> Shouldst rubies find: I by the tide
> Of Humber would complain...
> ...But at my back I always hear
> Time's winged chariot hurrying near.'

The part of the East Riding known as Holderness roughly extends east from the Wolds to the coast, and south from Bridlington to Spurn Head. Anyone wishing to gain some idea of the region in late Victorian and Edwardian times can do no better than read the novels of a writer who although born in the Doncaster area — where he also began his writing career — spent most of his life in the East Riding; then set out on a literary exploration of the region, comparing it in his time to that of today. Edward Charles Booth (1873-1954) wrote five novels and a book of short stories between 1908 and 1929, including *The Cliff End* (1908), *Fondie* (1916), *The Tree of the Garden* (1922) and *The Treble Clef* (1924). Today his work is largely neglected, though in his day he was well-known as a regional novelist, and his depiction of the East Riding was compared with Thomas Hardy's of 'Wessex' and even the novels of Dickens. Such eminent writers as the journalist Guy Schofield, the late Harry J Scott (founder of the *Dalesman*) and the topographical writer and lecturer S P B Mais firmly maintained that E C Booth's work merited a much larger readership.

He knew and loved the dialect and turns of phrase used in the area, and portrayed some remarkable characters in his books. Even for readers who cannot remember the days of the horse-drawn buses there is something nostalgic near the beginning of *The Cliff End* and the description of the journey of Tankard's horse-drawn bus. This two-horse vehicle, driven by its rather eccentric owner, regularly journeyed from Ullbrig to Hunmouth (Hull). On market days, farmers' wives travelled on it, laden with baskets of butter, eggs and other farm produce to sell in the city. Tankard had other business commitments apart from his bus, so down from his driver's seat he would clamber to depart on his appointed errand, regardless of his passengers. On his return he would declare:

'Ah'm fair sickened a't job. It's nowt bud clammerin' up and down t'bus side!'

Another notable character is Father Mostyn, the Anglican priest of Ullbrig, who tempers his religious message with a human touch characteristic of the region:

'Just call in at the vicarage as you would at the Ullbrig Arms;

you'll find the attention as good and the welcome greater. After eight o'clock you can be almost sure of catching me...'

According to one source, the figure of Father Mostyn was actually based on a former vicar of Aldborough, a village between Withernsea and Hornsea which provides the setting for the fictional town of Ullbrig.

His later novel *The Tree of the Garden* begins with the recently widowed Mrs John Openshaw hesitating before she opens her husband's roll-top desk. She does not like to pry into his affairs, even though she has emphatically told a friend: 'My husband told me everything.' On reading this, something takes seed in the reader's mind that there may be a secret lurking in that desk — and there is. Mrs Openshaw soon discovers from letters in the desk that her husband had a second family in another part of the city, and gallantly she goes to discover the woman who had secretly shared her husband's life for many years.

In 1924 *The Treble Clef* was published. Its young hero Oswald Holdroyd often has to go on errands for his mother to the more prosperous parts of the city. On one occasion he overhears the Mayor's imperious young daughter call him 'the sausage boy'. (Mrs Holdroyd has been forced to make a living selling meat pies and sausages after her husband's death.) This so infuriates him that he vows that one day he will become rich and powerful, and the novel tells of his struggle to achieve his ambition.

E C Booth died on the 6th July 1954 aged 81 at Scalby, Scarborough, where he had lived at 3 The Park with his brothers Bromley and George for many years. In a tribute to him after his death, the *Dalesman* wrote:

'His characterisation is executed with consummate skill, the result of penetrating observation; humour and irony, comedy and poignant tragedy being blended in a convincing picture of the rural life of the area...His titles...all carry an intensity of feeling packed with the very marrow of human interest.'

Hopefully his work will once again become as popular as it was during his day, offering as it does a vivid portrait of a vanished way of life in this picturesque part of Yorkshire.

Although one of Britain's most eminent modern poets, Philip Larkin (1922-1985) was a native of Coventry, the most important years of his life and work were while he was librarian at the Brynmor Jones Library of Hull University from 1955 until his death. Thirty years of influential and successful organising of an excellent library, yet he found time to produce some of the finest British poetry of this century, poetry that won him international fame. Amongst the awards he was granted during his lifetime were the Queen's Gold Medal for Poetry (1965) and the German Shakespeare Prize (1976).

He was born in 1922 in Coventry, where his father was city treasurer, and was educated at King Henry VIII Grammar School. His early ambition was to be a jazz drummer, and he retained his keen interest and knowledge in jazz all his life, reviewing records for prestigious magazines and newspapers — some of this is collected in his prose anthology, *All What Jazz* (1970).

His first taste of publication was in his school magazine. In 1940 he went up to St John's College, Oxford, to read English, where he was a contemporary of the novelist Kingsley Amis. As his short-sightedness prevented him being drafted during World War II, he became a librarian at Wellington in Shropshire. Later he moved to University College, Leicester and Queen's University, Belfast, before moving to the library at Hull University in 1955. He soon became a familiar figure locally, though he shunned personal publicity.

The North Ship (1945), his first collection of poems, and two novels had been published before he came to Yorkshire. The first, *Jill* (1946), concerned the experiences at Oxford of John Kemp, who was from a working-class Lancashire background. In order to give himself credibility in this strange new environment he implied that he had a younger sister called Jill who was at boarding school; complications occured when a real Jill turned up! The novel was regarded at the time as one of the better ones about university life in postwar years, portraying as it does the social changes taking place, especially within ancient institutions. His second novel, *A Girl in Winter* (1947), had a provincial library as its setting and concerned the experiences of a foreign girl, Kathleen, who worked there.

Philip Larkin's second collection of poems, *The Less Deceived* (1955), showed that he had found a distinctive poetic voice, based around lightly ironic and urbane verses, many with provincial settings. His work found a ready response in many readers not usually interested in modern poetry; in it they found experiences and events that corresponded to their own. Larkin often voiced his dislike for the 'modernist' school of poetry, feeling that its abstract and learned nature meant it was very difficult to understand by those who might otherwise read poetry. *The Whitsun Weddings,* his third collection, appeared in 1964, and ten years later *High Windows* was published. This last collection included *Going, Going,* one of his environmental poems familiar to those who might not otherwise regard themselves as readers of poetry. This particular poem was commissioned by the Department of the Environment, and a version of it appeared as *How Do You Want to Live?* (published by HMSO in 1972).

Philip Larkin also compiled *The Oxford Book of Twentieth Century English Verse* (1973), consisting of poems by the best-known of modern poets, as well as others which Larkin felt had been unduly neglected. Six poems by Hull-born Stevie Smith (1902-1971) were included (her family moved to London when she was small).

Philip Larkin died on the 2nd December 1985. A private funeral service was held at St Mary's Church, Cottingham, on the 9th December, and a public memorial service took place in Westminster Abbey in February 1986, when the Poet Laureate, Ted Hughes, was amongst the distinguished speakers. *An Enormous Yes: In Memorium of Philip Larkin* was published soon after his death, and it contained appreciations of the man and his work by many of his fellow writers and poets. In 1988 came his *Collected Poems,* edited by Anthony Thwaite, containing all his published work and also a number of previously unseen pieces.

The verdict of the literary experts is that he was one of the greatest modern poets in our language; the opinion of so many ordinary readers is that Philip Larkin's often slightly ironic poems express what they themselves feel about many aspects of modern life.

During his time as librarian, Larkin wrote *A Lifted Study-Storehouse:*

An Account of the Brynmor Jones Library 1929-1979 (1979). This was updated until 1985 by Maeve Brennan, a library colleague, as the first of the Philip Larkin Memorial Series. It contains virtually unaltered the whole of Larkin's original text and his foreword, and other pamphlets in the Memorial Series will be published by Hull University Press.

A novelist who set one of his historical works, *Mary Anerley: A Yorkshire Tale* (1880), in Flamborough was Richard Dodderidge Blackmore (1825-1900). He did not live in Yorkshire, but the county's coast, with its strong smuggling traditions, provided a fine subject he studied well. A meticulous writer, he maintained 'a page a day is my maximum'.

R D Blackmore was born on the 7th June 1825 at Longworth, Berkshire, where his father was curate-in-charge. After being educated at Blundell's School, Tiverton, and Exeter College, Oxford, he became a barrister in 1852 and then a schoolteacher. Illness forced him to take up a rural life, and he bought and ran a successful market garden at Teddington near London. Although Blackmore wrote fourteen novels, a book of short stories and seven books of verse, only a few of his novels are still read today. His first two novels were not successful, but the fact that one of Queen Victoria's daughters married the Marquis of Lorne in 1869 helped to rocket his *Lorna Doone* of the same year into the bestseller class. The reading public wrongly thought the story had something to do with the bridegroom's family history.

Mary Anerley is worth reading for its description of life in an eighteenth century Flamborough fishing village alone, but when coupled with a story in the best 'lost heir' tradition this is doubly true. Although caravans and holiday bungalows have changed part of Flamborough's appearance, it is still possible to visit many settings in this exciting story.

The hero is a foreign-looking waif who is brought to the village, and is named Robin after his rescuer. He grows up to be an adventurous smuggler whose haunts are still remembered in the name Robin Lyth Cave. Blackmore tells readers:

Phillip Larkin, poet and librarian at the Brynmor Jones Library, Hull University, reading a poem in public (a rare event) on the 30th September 1982 at the retirement presentation for Peter Sheldon, sub-librarian at the library, who also wrote the poem and can be seen sitting on the windowsill.

Winifred Holtby.

'It must not be thought that Flamborough although it was Robin's dwelling-place, so far as he had any — was the principal scene of his operations, the stronghold of his enterprises. On the contrary his liking was for the quiet caves, near Scarborough, and even to the north of Whitby when wind and tide were suitable.'

He is on the run from the coastguards when pretty Mary Anerley helps him to escape. So begins a romantic association that eventually ends happily, but not before Mary and Robin have experienced many problems. At one point Mary is sent to live for a time with her aunt at Filey, then still mainly a small fishing village, but one which has had its own literary associations as we shall see.

Mary's home, Anerley Farm, is situated 'in the clump of the space of the Wolds which hunks down at last into Flamborough Head'. The head itself is described as:

'The farthest forefront of a bare jagged coastline stretching boldly off to the eastwards, a strong rugged barrier. Away to the north, the land falls back into coves, bands and some straight lines.'

Of the Flamborough people, Blackmore wrote:

'The practice of Flamborough is to listen fairly to everything that might be said, and to receive it well in the crust of the mind and let it sink down. But even after that, it might not take root unless it were fixed in its settlement by their own two great powers, the Law and the Lord.'

Stephen Anerley, Mary's father, is a good example of a comfort-ably-off farmer of the time:

'Happy alike in the place of his birth, his lot in life and the wisdom of the powers appointed over him, he looked up with a substantial faith, yet a solid reserve of judgement to the Church, the Justices of the Peace, spiritual Lords and Temporal and above all His Majesty George the Third.

What he was brought up to, that he would abide by, and the sin beyond repentance to his mind, was the sin of the turncoat — he was kind and gentle and good to every one who knew how to behave himself.'

Obviously Robin, a smuggler and privateer, did not fall into the latter category, as the story reveals!

Compared to the industrial landscape of West Yorkshire, for example, the former East Riding has nurtured comparatively few world-famous writers, but ask any East Yorkshire inhabitant about their region's most famous author and the answer is likely to be Winifred Holtby (1898-1935).

Her life in, and associations with, East Yorkshire give the reader the chance to explore one of the most interesting literary landscapes in the whole county, covering an area from Hull and the Wolds right up the coast to Scarborough and Ravenscar. It includes Rudston, the village five miles west of Bridlington, where she was born on the 23rd June 1898 in Rudston House on Long Street, and in whose peaceful churchyard she is buried; the city of Hull, in whose reference library (now the library for local studies) she researched much of her most famous novel *South Riding;* Bridlington; historic Beverley; and Hornsea and Withernsea, which she combined to portray as Kiplington in *South Riding.*

Completed only a few weeks before her death on the 29th September 1935, *South Riding* was published in 1936. She had received the uncorrected typescript of the novel just before going into the London nursing home where she died, after a four year battle with Bright's Disease. *South Riding* was chosen as the March Book of the Month by the Book Society in 1936, and was awarded the James Tait Black Memorial Prize for the best novel of that year.

It has been said that a depressing evening spent with her old friend Harry Pearson of Driffield, the man she promised to marry just prior to her death, may have sparked off the story. The plot centres around problems and schemes connected with education, health, unemployment and housing, in addition to the intermingling of the private lives of the characters who crowd the novel. The strands of humour and compassion woven into the novel prove that Winifred Holtby knew and understood the people of the area, and of Yorkshire in general. It enabled her to create such memorable characters as Sarah Burton, the indomitable headmistress; Robert Carne, the impoverished landowner-farmer whose ancestors had owned his estate for over four hundred years; and the resourceful alderman, Mrs Beddows.

South Riding is written with a keen insight into the problems of the 1930's. According to Vera Brittain, Winifred Holtby's greatest friend:

'One of the main reasons for her plot was to show how local government with its apparently impersonal decisions affects the human histories of men and women.'

The plot owes much to the council work of Mrs Holtby, the first woman to be elected to the East Riding County Council in March 1923 and who later became an alderman. Winifred Holtby did not seek direct information from her mother, who would have probably refused to supply it. Instead she extracted old agendas of the East Riding County Council meetings from the dining room waste-paper basket after Mrs Holtby had gone to bed, and they provided some of the factual bones for the novel. Her 'Prefatory Letter' in *South Riding* addressed to her mother acknowledged some of the sources and expressed her admiration for her mother's work on the council.

David Holtby, Winifred's father, was a prosperous farmer in Rudston until agricultural problems in 1918 forced him to retire to Cottingham, just north of Hull, the following year. The sturdy Victorian house Bainesse was home to Winifred when she revisited the north — first from Oxford and then while living and working in London — and is now part of Hull University and has been renamed Holtby House. Cottingham itself never won her deep affection as her birthplace Rudston did. She fictionalised the latter as Anderby in *Anderby Wold,* published in 1923 and dedicated to her parents.

However, this was not her first published work. Even as a child she had been interested in making up stories and writing down her impressions. In December 1911 *My Garden and Other Poems* was published at her mother's expense as an unexpected Christmas gift, and to her great surprise the thirteen year old Winifred saw the book on sale just before Christmas. She never seems to have forgotten any of her early experiences, not even the bombardment of Scarborough and the east coast by warships of the German fleet in December 1914. At the time she was a boarder at Queen Margaret's School in the town, and wrote down her impressions which were later published in a Cumberland newspaper. She used the same event — which appalled Britain in the fourth month of World War I — in her novel *The Crowded Street* (1924).

In July 1918 she joined the Women's Auxiliary Army Corps as a private, but in October 1919 she returned to Somerville College, Oxford, which she had previously entered in October 1917. Here she and Vera Brittain met and became firm friends, and they encouraged each other as they both embarked on writing careers. They were both keen feminists, interested in social problems and the attempts to ensure world peace. Many of their articles appeared in the *Yorkshire Post*, in addition to publications including *Time and Tide*. Their friendship can be further explored in their correspondence in Vera Brittain's *Testament of Friendship* (1940) and in the Winifred Holtby Collection in Hull Library.

Just after the 1931 General Election, Winifred Holtby became ill. At first she was thought to be suffering from a nervous breakdown, but eventually her illness was diagnosed as Bright's Disease. Yet she still continued writing, lecturing and teaching, supported by medical aid and sheer willpower. In 1934 she rented a furnished cottage at Withernsea, and enjoyed the long walks towards Spurn Point. Keenly interested in her new surroundings, she noticed an old poster about a dancing display at the Withernsea's Floral Hall which later she used as the basis of the show given by Madame Hubbard's pupils in *South Riding*. The following year she lodged at Hornsea, collecting background material and working on her novel.

It is easy to visit many of the delightful places portrayed in *South Riding*. Beverley (Flintonbridge) is still a beautiful old town that has retained its character. It also influenced the description of picturesque Yarrold, a fictitious town set in South Holderness. The seaside town of Kiplington is a mixture of Hornsea and Withernsea with the latter's geographical situation. It is here that most of the novel is situated. Cold Harbour Colony is based on Sunk Island, not far from Withernsea and Winestead. (The latter was the setting for Maythorpe Hall, Robert Carne's home.) It was an ex-serviceman's settlement created after World War I on land that had been reclaimed from the sea over a hundred years previously.

Hull itself became Kingsport. It has changed with the replanning and rebuilding that had to be carried out after World War II, but many of the places she mentions in her novel still exist. Albion Street was the model for Willoughby Place, where Lily Sawdon, wife of the landlord of the Nag's Head between Maythorpe and Cold Harbour, went to consult Dr Stretton and learned that she did not have long to live — something she had feared.

But the beginning and the end of any exploration of Winifred Holtby country must be Rudston. It is here that she was born and spent her formative years on her parents' farm, and it is here that she is buried at the west end of the churchyard. A carved book on her grave bears the words:

'Give me work till my life shall end,
And life till my work is done.'

Surely she was granted this. Inside the church, near the font, is a memorial tablet giving details of her life and death. It was erected by the Winifred Holtby Society and states amongst other things that 'her work was notable for understanding, insight and sincerity'. In recent years the filming of her most famous work has helped to show a wider public what a fine novelist this daughter of the Yorkshire Wolds became.

Many novelists have enjoyed staying in Scarborough, the picturesque seaside town about fifteen miles further up the coast from Rudston and Bridlington. One of the earliest visitors was the Scottish-born Tobias Smollett (1721-1771), who pursued a varied career as novelist, doctor, dramatist and traveller. He described the spa town in his *Humphry Clinker* (1771), an epistolatory novel — so called because the story takes the form of letters between the various characters — about a journey round the country by Matthew Bramble, accompanied by members of his family and Humphry Clinker himself, Matthew's postilion or carriage-driver. Leaving London for the north, they travel via Harrogate to Scarborough, where Humphry rescues his naked master from the sea while he is bathing, and the party feel it wise to leave the next day. Smollett was not impressed with the town itself, though he admired its setting:

'Scarborough, though a paltry town is romantic from the situation along the Cliff that over-hangs the sea. The harbour is formed by a natural break, directly opposite to the town, and on that section is the castle, which stands very high...'

Although the Brontë family are synonymous with Haworth and the West Riding, it is not true to assume that they spent all their time isolated there. Both Charlotte and Emily studied for a time in Brussels, and all three sisters were governesses at one time or another in various parts of Yorkshire. It is interesting to look at their seaside visits in this chapter.

Ellen Nussey had written to her old school friend Charlotte Brontë (1816-1855), suggesting the idea of a joint visit to the coast, and on the 26th July 1839 Charlotte replied:

'Your proposal has almost driven me 'clean daft' — an excursion with you anywhere — just by ourselves would be delightful. The idea of seeing the sea — of being near it — watching its changes by sunrise, sunset, moonlight and noon-day, in calm perhaps in storm, fills and satisfies my mind.'

Charlotte's home conditions did not make the arrangements easy. Both Mr Brontë and aunt Branwell, who had come from Cornwall after Mrs Brontë's death in 1821, seemed reluctant for her to go, but by the 4th August, consent had been given. In mid-September Charlotte and Ellen set off for the east coast. At first they had planned to lodge in Bridlington, but Ellen's brother, Henry Nussey, had arranged for them to stay with his friends Mr and Mrs Hudson of Easton House Farm, two miles inland from the coast. (Henry Nussey had been curate at Burton Agnes, about five miles south-west of Bridlington.) Charlotte was so moved by her first view of the sea that she began to cry, and had to rest for a while before going on.

The Hudsons arranged that the last week of the ladies' holiday be spent in Bridlington itself, in lodgings on the cliff opposite the pier, now the esplanade. On returning home after her holiday, Charlotte wrote to thank Henry Nussey for the arrangements he had made and stated that:

Rudston House, where Winifred Holtby lived as a child.

A lithograph of Cliff Bridge and South Bay, c.1845.

Charlotte Brontë's watercolour of her sister Anne from June 1834.

Anne Brontë's grave in St Mary's churchyard. The bottom of the barbican of Scarborough Castle can be seen on the extreme right.

Cliff Bridge and Wood's Lodgings on St Nicholas' Cliff, c.1860. Charlotte, Anne and Ellen Nussey stayed in Wood's Lodgings on Anne's final visit before her death in May 1849.

'...the glories of the sea, the sound of its restless waves, formed a subject for contemplation that never wearied either the eye, the ear or the mind.'

Anne, the youngest of the Brontës, born 1820, set the ending of her novel *Agnes Grey* (1847) at Scarborough, where she had enjoyed holidays while governess between 1841 and 1845 with the Robinson family at Thorp Green Hall in Little Ouseburn, north-east of Knaresborough. Her first visit was when the Robinsons took furnished rooms in 'the best part of town', St Nicholas' Cliff. Anne was delighted with the sea and the castle towering over North and South Bay. She wrote:

'Refreshed, delighted, invigorated, I walked along forgetting all my cares, feeling as if I had wings on my feet, and could go at least forty miles without fatigue, and experiencing a sense of invigoration to which I had been an entire stranger since the days of early youth...the sea was my delight.'

While Anne was governess at Thorp Green Hall, the Rev William Weightman, her father's curate, died of cholera on the 6th September 1842. She had been in love with this charming, versatile young man who had been such a good influence on the wayward Branwell. He became the model for the Rev E Weston in *Agnes Grey*. Anne had already begun to write 'Passages in the Life of an Individual' in 1842, based on her own experiences as a governess with two families — the Robinsons, and previously Mrs Ingham at Blake Hall, Mirfield in West Yorkshire. Eventually her heroine provided the title of her novel *Agnes Grey,* published in 1847 under the pseudonym Acton Bell (it will be remembered that Charlotte was Currer Bell, and Emily, Ellis Bell).

Just as in Anne's life, Agnes's romance did not go smoothly: Mr Weston left his curacy; Agnes and her mother set up a school at Scarborough (the author's idea of an earthly paradise); but she could not forget him:

'I could think of him day and night. I could feel that he was worthily to be thought of. Nobody could love him as I could if I might.'

However, one day Agnes unexpectedly meets Mr Weston walking across the Scarborough sands at low tide, and they walk together through the town — though he is very serious and seems distracted. Only when they come within site of the old church of St Mary's and Castle Hill 'with the deep blue sea beyond did Mr Weston become cheerful'. He had waited to propose marriage 'in a high and noble setting'. Agnes agrees to marry him, and towards the end of the novel she records:

'I shall never forget that glorious summer evening, and always remember with delight that steep hill, and the edge of the precipice where we stood together, watching the splendid sunset mirrored in the restless world of water at our feet.'

Anne's own life ended very differently, but in quiet peace and joy in the Scarborough she loved so much. After Emily's death in December 1848, Anne began to decline in health too. She was an easier patient than her strong-minded sister (who would never consent to being regarded as ill), but one determined to visit Scarborough again. Her last wish was granted, and Charlotte, Ellen Nussey and Anne set off on the 24th May 1849, breaking their journey at York. They stayed at Wood's Lodgings, 2 The Cliff, now part of the Grand Hotel site. Charlotte wrote:

'Our lodgings are pleasant. As Anne sits by the window she can look at the sea, which this morning is as calm as glass.'

Ellen related how her spirits were high as she drove on the sands for an hour and:

'...lest the poor donkey should be urged to a greater speed than her heart thought right, she took the reins and drove herself.'

Sadly Anne died on the 28th May. In a letter to Mr Williams of the publishers Smith Elder, Charlotte tells of Anne's death, and how the doctor had been impressed with her 'fortitude and readiness to die'. There were plans to take the body back to Haworth, but Charlotte decided 'to lay the flower in the place where it had fallen'. Because St Mary's Church near the castle was undergoing restoration from October 1848 until July 1850, Anne's funeral service was held at Christ's Church, Vernon Road, though she was buried in St Mary's churchyard. After Anne's funeral, Ellen left for home and Charlotte moved to Easton Farm once again. Here she stayed until late June

1849 and consoled herself by working on the manuscript of her novel *Shirley* which she had brought with her.

The majority of visitors to ancient St Mary's still go into the graveyard to see Anne's grave. Few notice, however, that her age is wrongly inscribed on the headstone — it reads as 28 when it should be 29. This was the reason for Charlotte's subsequent visit to Scarborough in 1852 when, as she wrote on the 23rd June of that year:

'I have visited the churchyard, seen the stone, there were five errors, consequently I had to give directions for its being re-faced and re-lettered.'

She then went on to stay at Cliff House, Filey, 'but in less expensive rooms' than she and Ellen occupied after Anne's death.

By the time of her later visit in 1852, the little resort of Filey was becoming more popular, and new lodging houses and hotels were being built to accommodate the growing number of visitors. Charlotte records, however, that she often only saw seabirds and fishing boats as she strolled on the beach.

Although it is easy to trace where she stayed, it is not so easy to follow her to the neglected little church she attended one Sunday. She described it as:

'...not more than thrice the length and breadth of our passage, floored in brick, the walls green with time and decay. At one end there is a little gallery for the singers and when these personages stood up to perform they turned their backs on pulpit and parson.'

Was it Muston Church she attended? According to the Hunmanby historian, Lucy M Owston, Muston did possess a very neglected church at this time which was completely rebuilt in 1863. Wherever it was, it afforded Charlotte some amusement.

Neither Charlotte nor Anne stated any preference for either North or South Bay at Scarborough, unlike the youthful Compton Mackenzie (1883-1972) who stayed at Scarborough in September 1893, as he tells in the second volume of his ten volume autobiography *My Life and Times* (1963-1971). His parents were appearing at the Spa Theatre at the time. He loved the north side of the resort more than the south, and one reason for this was that in his opinion North Bay donkeys were much livelier than their South Bay counterparts. He also decided that the resort was 'two seaside places in one', a verdict probably shared by many of its visitors. The narrow arcade that ran along one side of the Spa Theatre and Concert Hall also fascinated him — its little shops sold delicious sweets, including popcorn, which he regarded as a Scarborough speciality. Sir Compton's visits were happy boyhood memories; one to the cricket festival week when he saw the famous Yorkshire bowler of the time, Peel, was an experience he never forgot even many years later.

A family of writers who knew Scarborough as part of their everyday lives were the Sitwells. Osbert Sitwell (1892-1969) was born in London, but baptised at Scarborough's St Mary's Church in 1893. His sister Edith (1887-1964), later Dame Edith, and their younger brother Sacheverell (1897-1988) were born in Scarborough, the former at Wood End, the latter at Belvoir House. Wood End, a large mansion on the Crescent was bought by the widowed Lady Louisa Sitwell, their grandmother, in 1870. Her son George was only ten years old when the family came to live in the house, so both he, and later his own children Osbert, Edith and Sacheverell, were very familiar with the resort.

After Wood End was given to Sir George by Lady Louisa, he built the library wing and the connecting bridge across the conservatory. He left an account of the exotic birds that frequented the conservatory, and also his impressions of life in late nineteenth century Scarborough. His idiosyncratic personality lives on in the autobiographical volumes of his son Osbert.

Sir George would probably never have regarded writing as a career, and in fact when it came to choosing a profession for his son, Sir George decided that it would be a good thing for Osbert to enter the town clerk's office. According to Sir Osbert's third volume of auto-biography, *Great Morning* (1948), he was to:

'...start at the bottom and climb right up to the top — the top consisting I inferred as being town clerk of Scarborough.'

What is more, he had to study commercial subjects under a specially-engaged tutor at Renishaw Hall, their Derbyshire mansion.

The Sitwell Family by J S Sargent (1900). Sir George wrote in March of that year: 'Sargent's picture is going on famously and I think it will be finished in a fortnight. We are all very much pleased with it. Lady Ida is standing in a silver and white evening dress arranging flowers in that old silver bowl on a little first Empire table. Osbert and the baby [Sacheverell] are on the floor to her left, giving the black pug a biscuit. I am standing to her right in dark grey and with brown riding boots with one hand on Edith's shoulder — she is in scarlet. The tapestry and old French chiffonier make a most satisfactory background. We have put Lady Ida in a black ''shadow'' hat, something like that in Copley's picture, with white feathers and red ribbons...'

Alan Ayckbourn.

However, Osbert became a soldier in the Grenadier Guards and soon afterwards came World War I. Scarborough never had one of the Sitwells to help rule its municipal affairs.

The German bombardment of the resort on the 16th December 1914 did, however, provide Sir Osbert with the subject of his novel *Before the Bombardment* (1926). Set in Newborough (Scarborough), it depicted the effect of the raid and its aftermath on the town's genteel population. It was enjoyed by many readers because of its satirical portrayal of some of the town's residents, and so did not find favour in local circles.

Some of Sir Osbert's short stories were also set in Scarborough, most notably *Low Tide* and the spine-chilling *A Place of One's Own*. The latter takes place in the early part of this century when the Smedhursts, a retired Leeds couple, decide to occupy Bellingham House (based on Wood End), the former home of a Miss Bezyre. They are a little puzzled why such a desirable residence has been empty so long. Then they are even more puzzled once they move in when they hear a disembodied voice echoing through the speaking tube system, when they know that there is no-one in the room from which it came. Then...

Early in the story is a fine description of Newborough's seaside atmosphere of summer crowds, 'hokey-pokey' sellers and banana vendors — then a novelty fruit. (A film of *A Place of One's Own* starring the Huddersfield-born actor James Mason was made in 1945.)

Just after World War I and before he embarked on his career as an author, Captain Osbert Sitwell, as he then was, stood as Liberal candidate for the Scarborough constituency. One place he had to canvass was Robin Hood's Bay ten miles up the coast, where he noticed that the best villas were owned by 'whole groups of Sea Captains, retired'. He came second, defeated by the Conservative candidate, but declared that he had enjoyed the contest. In order to be right in the heart of his constituency, once again he lived at Wood End, which had been unused for several years after 1914. In 1925 Sir George Sitwell closed the mansion altogether, and nine years later he sold it to Scarborough Corporation. It is now a fine museum of natural history and geology, but the library wing contains portraits and books relating to the Sitwell family.

Many of the town's other fine buildings have been utilised for other purposes than their original ones. One such is the former Victorian Boys High School, overlooking Valley Gardens. In 1976 it was transformed into the new home of Scarborough's Theatre-in-the-Round.

When this pioneer company was founded in 1953 by Stephen Joseph, son of the publisher Michael Joseph and the actress Hermione Gingold, it was housed in the central library. He had chosen this north-eastern seaside town for this new venture because at the time London 'seemed hopeless economically'. The new theatre's reputation increased rapidly, especially after Alan Ayckbourn's first plays were produced there. But Ackbourn had at first joined the company as stage manager, not a playwright.

The year 1959 brought the production of his first play — the result of a challenge laid down by Stephen Joseph. At the time Ayckbourn had complained about a character in a play. The director suggested that he should write one himself, and if it was good he would ensure it was performed. Written under the pseudonym of Roland Allen, that first play *The Square Cat* was the summer season production of 1959. From then until the present day, Ayckbourn has launched thirty-two of his plays from Scarborough. Most have gone on to be West End successes; many have been translated into several languages and performed abroad. In 1985 he captured every major award for his National Theatre production of *A Chorus of Disapproval,* premiered in Scarborough in 1984. Even though he is London-born, in Hampstead on the 12th April 1939, he claims he has adopted Yorkshire. Nobody can deny that Yorkshire has adopted him — and is determined to make the literary and theatrical world realise this.

His father was leader of the London Symphony Orchestra and his mother a writer of stories for women's magazines. He has said that she had bought him a small typewriter to keep him quiet as a child, and on it he had 'banged out derivative adventures'. After leaving Haileybury School at seventeen, he joined a theatre company as an assistant stage manager, which meant he had to be versatile. During his career he has been at various times a stage manager, sound technician, lighting technician, scene painter, prop maker, actor, BBC radio drama producer in Leeds, writer and director. He now concentrates on the latter two roles, and since 1976 has been artistic director of the Stephen Joseph Theatre-in-the-Round.

Why are his plays so popular? Undoubtedly one reason is his keen ear for the way people speak, as he said in 1964:

'I have a love of England's colloquial language, its flexibility. No one word means any one thing. Everything is rife with misinterpretation.'

Then there is his perceptive comment in *The Times* in 1982:

'Mainly I want to say things about the fear and distrust people have for each other, the fact that men and women still don't seem to understand each other very well.'

Ayckbourn shows there is a very fine line between comedy and tragedy, and that the two genres have much in common. In writing his plays he allows the characters to take over to a certain extent, and gives a vivid example of this in an interview with the *New York Times* in 1979:

'The characters have to be allowed to control their own destinies. I sometimes say to one of them ''I wish you'd leave the stage, because that would give me a nice, neat ending.'' And he refuses to go, and then end is bungled. But then you find you're left with something much more interesting.'

One of Ayckbourn's most famous plays, *Time and Time Again,* is in sequence the eleventh of his full-length plays, and has been translated into twenty-four different languages. It was first performed in Scarborough in July 1971, made its London debut at the Comedy Theatre in August 1972, and was adapted for television on the 18th May 1976. The author describes it:

'The play invites us to explore the role of an eternal quadrangle. A girl and three men. One man she wants, one she used to want and one she doesn't want at any price. The one she doesn't want, doesn't want her associating with the one she does want, whilst the one she used to want mistakenly thinks she wants the one she doesn't want. As for the one she wants — he doesn't know what he wants!'

That description gives an insight into a style of dramatic humour which appeals to millions the world over. Both reading Ayckbourn's plays and seeing them performed brings a realisation that he has succeeded in giving new life to the often jaded theatrical genres, and is rightly one of the most popular and successful playwrights in the world today. He has never been content to rest on his laurels, however. He is constantly striving to keep his plays as sharp and witty as they have always been, and for 'new ways of making comedy more truthful — and strange as it may seem, more meaningful'.

The small fishing village of Robin Hood's Bay has not changed much over the last fifty years, except perhaps in the increased number of visitors in the summer, many of whom first discover it in the writings of its most famous literary son, Leo Walmsley (1892-1966), and have come to see the bay for themselves. Although born in the West Riding town of Shipley, his family moved to Robin Hood's Bay when he was quite young, so that his father Ulric could more successfully pursue his career as an artist. The family, with three boys and a girl, lived in a house in King Street, now adorned by a blue plaque informing passers-by that Leo Walmsley once lived here.

Leo attended the local school and later Scarborough Secondary School (now the Theatre-in-the-Round). In his spare time he often went fishing, at first with home-made tackle, played amongst the fishing cobles and noted the rivalry that often cropped up between the old bay fisherman and the 'offcumuns'. He absorbed so much of the day-to-day life here in his youth that it was natural this would provide him with the basis for many of his later novels and stories.

After leaving school, he was briefly a teacher, then an assistant at the marine research station set up by Leeds University at Robin Hood's Bay where he worked alongside a young man, Sam Wilson, who became one of his greatest friends. During World War I he served in the Royal Flying Corps and was decorated for bravery. Later life overseas provided him with material for stories and articles published in many well-known journals of the day. But it was not until he

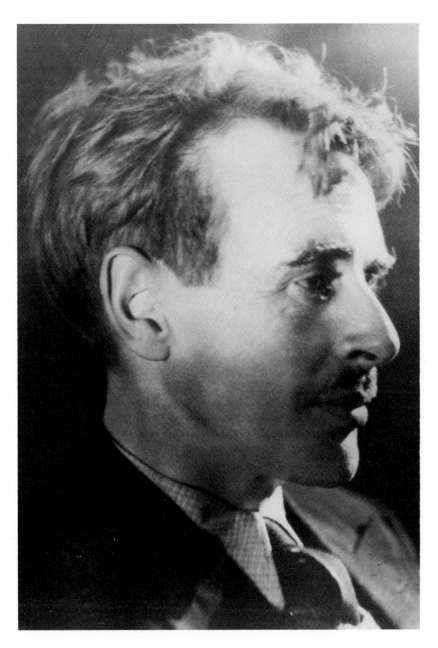

Leo Walmsley.

A picture by the eminent Victorian photographer Frank Meadow Sutcliffe of some of the fishermen Leo Walmsley knew — the Storm family on the beach with their coble Gratitude.

An early view of Whitby Bridge taken by Frank Meadow Sutcliffe.

transformed Robin Hood's Bay into Bramblewick and Whitby into Burnharbour that his career really took off.

Such novels as *Three Fevers* (1932) — filmed as *The Turn of the Tide* and premiered at the Picture House, Whitby — *Phantom Lobster* (1933), *Foreigners* (1935) and *Sally Lunn* (1937) relate something of the lives and work of the fisherfolk of the area as they battle against nature to eke out a livelihood for themselves. Of his autobiographical works, often classed as semi-autobiographical, *So Many Loves* (1944) deals especially with his life in Robin Hood's Bay; the others, *Love in the Sun* (1939), *The Golden Waterwheel* (1954) and *Paradise Creek* (1963) are mainly set in Fowey in Cornwall or Wales.

Leo Walmsley described Robin Hood's Bay:

'It lay compact in a ravine whose north-east side was the protecting sea cliffs, and its cottages were so closely packed together the tiled roofs were almost continuous, making a great blotch of red slightly varied by a pearly haze of smoke...'

From their first publication, local people have often advised visitors who wish to gain a true impression of the area to read his novels. Now many already know something of the background of a writer whose recipe for the training of a novelist was:

'...living, doing things, exploring, but not necessarily far from home. Above all observing places and people first hand.'

This is a rule he himself certainly lived up to, and it is fascinating to read his novels and then set out on one's own literary exploration to discover their settings, the lifestyles he portrays and the associations that influenced him. It certainly provides one of the most interesting explorations of a 'literary landscape', as Robin Hood's Bay is still very similar in appearance to that of his day.

A five mile journey up the East Yorkshire coastline brings us to the old whaling port of Whitby, which has attracted many authors and poets, several of whom set their work in the district. Essentially it has changed little over the years, so it is quite easy to follow in their footsteps.

The port's pioneer poet was the Saxon cowherd Caedmon (fl 670), the first English poet whose identity we know for certain. According to the Northumberland ecclesiastical historian the Venerable Bede, Caedmon fell asleep near his cattle. A voice requested him to sing something. Caedmon refused. He knew he was no singer, besides, what could he sing about? 'Sing about the beginning of Creation', the voice urged. Caedmon obeyed, and to his amazement later he could repeat all he had sung in his dream. *The Song of Creation,* credited to him, has a foremost place in early English literature.

Supposedly encouraged by Abbess Hilda, he became aware that he had been called on to compose religious poetry. He became a monk at the abbey of Streoneshalh (Whitby) — founded in 657 by the Northumbrian king Oswy — and spent his remaining years writing peoms based on the Bible and other religious subjects.

He would no doubt be astounded to see the thousands of present-day visitors climbing the 199 steps (though John Wesley miscounted them as being 198), and pausing to examine the cross erected in his honour situated close to the abbey — though this is a ruin of a much later building than the one Caedmon knew. Its site is impressive, standing high on the cliff to the east of the port it overlooks. Canon Rawnsley, one of the founders of the National Trust, was instrumental in starting the scheme to commemorate Caedmon here. The cross was unveiled by the Poet Laureate of the time, Leeds born Alfred Austin.

The previous Poet Laureate, Alfred Lord Tennyson (1809-1892), loved to explore Whitby. He had been appointed Poet Laureate on the 19th November 1850, largely he believed because the Prince Consort so admired his poem *In Memoriam,* written after the death of his friend Arthur Hallam. Tennyson was staying at 5 North Terrace, which later became part of the Royal Hotel, when he wrote to his wife on the 8th July 1852:

'I am set down here for a week at least in lodgings. It is rather a fine place, a river running into the sea between precipices; on one side new buildings and a very handsome hotel belonging to Hudson, the Railway King; on the other side at the very top a gaunt old Abbey and older Parish church hanging out over the town and hundreds of white gravestones that looked to my eye, something like clothes laid out to dry.'

There was an election in progress at the time, and Tennyson was intrigued to witness the noise and flag-waving of the crowds. These included men he described as 'Northern boatmen of Danish breed, who meet and hug each other for the love of liberty', and what he called the 'foolish fellows'.

During his beach and cliff explorations he noticed some beautiful little ammonites which he tried to dislodge, but discovered they were embedded in the rock. He was still enjoying his holiday — and, as he reported, reading many novels — when he wrote again to his wife on the 19th July:

'I have ordered a carriage and am going to see Lord Normanby's park near here [on the outskirts of Sandsend] — I met an old smuggler on the coast yesterday who had been in Lord Normanby's service (not as a smuggler of course) and he took me for Lord Normanby at first, a likeness I have been told of more than once before. I got into conversation with him and I am going to call for him to-day and he is to show me the caves and holes where they used to hide their kegs.'

It was not smugglers but the old whaling fleet that brought Mrs Elizabeth Gaskell (1810-1865) to Whitby. Born in Chelsea, the daughter of a Unitarian minister, she was brought up by her aunt in Knutsford, Cheshire. In 1848 she had written *Mary Barton,* and, encouraged by Dickens, had gone on to pursue a career as a novelist with such books as *Cranford* (1853), *Ruth* (1853) and *North and South* (1855). As the author of *The Life of Charlotte Brontë* we will meet her again in chapter four.

She and her daughters Julia and Meta came to stay for a week or ten days at 1 Abbey Terrace, West Cliff. From here she set out to research the background of the old press gangs who used to swoop down on the fishing villages and ports, and carry off any strong men they could find to serve in the Royal Navy.

Out of painstaking enquiries and detailed studies Mrs Gaskell created *Sylvia's Lovers,* one of her finest novels, published in 1863. Her knowledge of whaling and its dangers was mainly derived from Dr William Scoresby. Like his father, who had invented the crow's nest as a lookout point on ships, the younger William had been captain of a whaler before being ordained and becoming Vicar of Bradford Parish Church (now the cathedral).

Set during the Napoleonic Wars, the author gives a vivid picture of a press gang attacking homecoming sailors in Monkshaven (Whitby) who have landed from Greenland. Sylvia Robson and her friend Molly are buying a length of material for a new cloak in Foster's shop, Bridge Street, when:

'...Hark!

No one spoke, no one breathed; I had almost said, no heart beat for listening. Not long; in an instant there rose a sharp tumultaneous cry of many people in rage and despair. Inarticulate at that distance, it was yet an intelligible curse, and the roll, and the roar, and the irregular tramp came nearer and nearer.

'They're taking 'em to t' Randvause', said Molly. 'Eh! I wish I'd King George here just to tell him my mind.'

The girl clenched her hands, and set her teeth.

'It's terrible hard!' said Hester, 'there's mothers and wives looking out for 'em as if they were stars dropt out o't lift.'

'But what can we do for 'em?' cried Sylvia, 'Let us go into t'thick and do a bit of helpin'; I can't stand quiet and see 't.'

Half-crying, she pushed towards the door but Philip held her back.

'Sylvia! You must not. Don't be silly; it's the law, and no one can do aught against it — least of all women and lasses.'

By this time, the vanguard of the crowd came pressing up Bridge Street, past the windows of Foster's shop...'

As a word-picture of old Whitby, the novel is outstanding. Some of its characters, such as John and Jeremiah Foster, Quaker drapers and bankers, give a real insight into the commercial life of the time. It is still possible to explore the settings, especially those around East Cliff. (Much of West Cliff had yet to be built upon at the time of the story.) Even if the actual buildings have been removed or renovated, glimpses of the old seaport are easy to discover. These help to remind readers of the times when the arrival of the returning whaling fleet after a twelve month voyage was of supreme importance to the inhabitants of Whitby and their future prosperity.

Mrs Elizabeth Gaskell.

Modern-day Whitby.

Around Whitby is farming land and Sylvia herself is brought up on her parents' farm. The illustrator of *Sylvia's Lovers,* Gerald Du Maurier, had written to a friend who was bringing young children with him on holiday:

'Tell them to walk over the cliffs westward, through fields and over stiles until they reach Sylvia's cottage...'

The novel's plot concerns the deceit perpetrated by Philip Hepburn, former upright assistant at Fosters, who is so much in love with his young cousin Sylvia Robson that he is consumed by jealousy when he notices her attraction to Charley Kinraid, the specksioneer (harpooner) of a Hartlepool whaler. After seeing Kinraid hustled away by a press gang in a lonely cove eight miles from Monkshaven — this in spite of whaling being a Government-protected calling — Philip fails to pass on Kinraid's message to Sylvia. Soon after, Kinraid's white hat with a piece of Sylvia's distinctive hair ribbon fastened inside is found on the beach. Everyone presumes he has drowned, and Philip does nothing to contradict them. Inevitably, Kinraid returns to Monkshaven a year later, now a well-regarded member of the Royal Navy. He has come back to claim his sweetheart, only to discover she is now married to Philip.

Much has happened during his absence. Sylvia's father Daniel Robson, a farmer, has endeavoured to save other young men from the press gang by leading an attack on, and then setting fire to, the press gang's Monkshaven headquarters, the Marriner's Arms. On that occasion, press officers had used the fire alarm bell as a decoy to bring men into the streets, and many were captured for the navy. Daniel, a former sailor himself, had pointed out to his supporters:

'But when we seven lies out and rouses t'town ther'll be many a score ready to grant to t'Marriner's Arms and it'll be easy work reskeyin' them chaps as is pressed. Us seven each man-Jack on us, go and seek his friends — then maybe there'll be some theere as'll not be so soft as we was lettin' them poor chaps be carried off from under our noses: just because our ears were busy listenin' to yon confounded bell, whose clip-clopping tongue a'll tear out afore this week is out...'

Unfortunately the rescue fails, and Daniel is caught, tried and hanged at York for leading the attack. (Mrs Gaskell based this attack on an event that actually took place around nine o'clock on the 26th February 1796 on the house of John Cooper, the rendezvous for the press gang officers.) In dire straits after her father's death and Charley's disappearance, Sylvia has been forced to marry Philip. When Charley returns, however, Sylvia recognises her husband's dishonesty and he is forced to flee. He eventually comes back, and Sylvia now grants him her forgiveness before he finally dies.

Though the latter part of the novel contains many last-minute reconciliations and happily resolved endings of the kind so favoured by Victorian writers, the book is still an impressive evocation of what life was like two centuries ago in a small fishing port when everyone was dependent on one industry for their livelihood.

Two years after Mrs Gaskell's stay at Whitby, another renowned author visited the town in August 1861. Wilkie Collins (1824-1889) had a pleasant room overlooking the sea, but complained that the hotel band disturbed him from writing. Perhaps his annoyance can be excused when we remember that after ten years as a novelist he had found fame with the publication of *The Woman in White* (1860), which had previously been serialised in Dickens's periodical *All the Year Round.* During his Whitby visit he was no doubt concerned to preserve the high reputation he had achieved with this book, and others such as *No Name* (1862) and *Armadale* (1866), as a master of the mystery story. He had also begun to suffer from a variety of ailments, including arthritis and gout, and, like many people in the eighteenth and nineteenth centuries, took small doses of laudanum or opium — freely available in those days from any druggists — to relieve the pain and to which in time he became addicted.

Although it is not known for certain what Collins was writing during his Whitby visit, he did set much of his novel *The Moonstone* on the lonely coastline between Whitby and Scarborough. First published, again after serialisation, in 1868, the book is regarded as one of the earliest detective stories in English literature. Collins's self-declared aim was an attempt 'to trace the influence of character on circumstances'.

The Moonstone centres around a large and valuable diamond known as the moonstone. An introductory chapter relates how this was stolen from an image of an Indian god by an Englishman often called 'the wicked colonel', great-uncle of the heroine Rachel Verrinder. The stone is believed to bring disaster to anyone who unlawfully possesses it, and as the novel unfolds this prediction is borne out.

The story is told by seven characters, each offering a different perspective on the events that happen to them. (Collins was well-known for his ability to construct original plots and used a variety of narrative techniques.) One of them is the opium addict, Ezra Jennings, the doctor's assistant, and his comments on the effects of the drug can only have come from Collins's own experience. One of the most interesting narrators is the old Yorkshire house steward, Gabriel Betteredge. When perplexed by any problem, large or small, he believed in sitting down with a pipeful of tobacco and dipping into *Robinson Crusoe,* as some people might seek guidance from the Bible. He certainly had plenty of opportunity to exercise his agile brain, for as soon as the moonstone is given to Rachel as an eighteenth birthday legacy from her wicked uncle, strange things begin to happen in the lonely Yorkshire home, as well as the family's London residence. Betteredge comments:

'...here was our quiet English house suddenly invaded by a devilish Indian diamond — bringing after it a conspiracy of living rogues set loose on us by the living vengeance of a dead man — whoever heard the like of it...'

The old steward continues:

'Our house is right up on the Yorkshire coast by the sea. We have got beautiful walks all round in every direction but one. That I acknowledge to be a horrid walk. It leads for a quarter of a mile through a melancholy plantation of firs; and brings you out between low cliffs on the loneliest little bay on all our coast.

The same hills run down to the sea and end in two spits of rocks — jutting out opposite each other — between the two, shifting backwards and forwards at certain seasons of the year lies the most horrible quicksands on the shores of Yorkshire.'

It is the hunchbacked servant Rosanna Spearman, who was once imprisoned for theft, who deliberately walks on to the 'shivering sands' to her death; she feared that Detective Sergeant Cuff, who is investigating the mysterious crime, might accuse her of the moonstone's disappearance.

In his book *The Great North Road* (1961), Frank Morley suggested to visitors travelling eastwards from the Vale of Pickering towards Robin Hood's Bay:

'...if you wish, spend a little time at the detective work required to identify precisely, the location of the shivering sands which are of unforgettable importance to anyone who has read Wilkie Collins's story *The Moonstone.* '

It is up to the reader to try and discover whether such sands really exist; or were they either simply a fictitious stretch of beach or the result of the unsteady gaze of the author?

Many Americans over the years have enjoyed holidays in Whitby. One of the resort's greatest admirers in the last century was the American poet and essayist James Russell Lowell (1819-1891), who spent a month or six weeks here nearly every year from 1880 to 1889. Born in Cambridge, Massachusetts, the son of a minister, he graduated from Harvard and from 1843 he edited the journal *The Pioneer,* with Hawthorne and Edgar Allen Poe as contributors. In 1855 he was made a professor at Harvard and came to Europe as part of his research. In 1877 he became American minister in Spain, and at the time of his first visit to Whitby he was the newly appointed minister to England, a position he held from 1880 to 1885. The artist George Du Maurier, who had stayed in Whitby in order to illustrate *Sylvia's Lovers,* had recommended the old sea port to him as an ideal holiday place.

Like many other visitors, Lowell and his wife first stayed at the Royal Hotel. Later they moved to the Misses Galilee at 3 Wellington Terrace. At that time Mrs Lowell was in poor health, and her husband used to take her for long excursions in an invalid chair, hoping that the bracing sea air would restore her strength. After her death he still continued his Whitby visits, and in his last recorded impression he tells how 'the moors and shy footpaths around here are dearer to me than ever'.

On the 18th August 1887 he wrote to a friend, Miss Sedgewick in London:

'I am really at Whitby; whither I have been every summer but '85 for the last six years. This will tell you how much I like it. A very primitive place it is, and the manners and ways of its people, much like those of New England.

Tis a wonderfully picturesque place with the bleaching bones of the Abbey standing aloof on the cliff and dominating the area.'

He went on to describe the 'yards', steep flights of stone steps hurrying down from East and West Cliff to the river side, and also how small girls would take family pies to be baked in the large oven at the local bakery. He adds:

'And I wish you could see the pier with its throng of long-booted fishermen looking like worthy descendants of the Norsemen who first rowed their ships under the shelter of the cliffs...'

Lowell often wrote poetry while he was staying here, and in 1889 wrote *The Brook*. On his return to London he found a letter and a cheque from a publisher for any poem he might care to send, so he posted his Whitby-written one.

Whitby is proud of its own nineteenth century author. In 1884 Mary Linskill (1840-1891) saw the publication of *Between the Heather and the Northern Sea,* the first of her popular Whitby-based novels. The second, *The Haven Under the Hill,* appeared in 1887. She was already a published writer, using the pseudonym Stephen Yorke for her work.

Mary Linskill was born in a cottage along Blackburn's Yard, off Church Street on East Cliff. Her father, amongst other jobs, was one of the town's constables. An interest in reading from an early age led her to hope that one day she might be able to make a living as a writer. This must have been a distant hope, however, when she left school at twelve years old and was apprenticed as a milliner in Charles Wilson's shop at the east end of the bridge. Later she moved to Manchester and then Newcastle-under-Lyme. As her first trade did not suit her ambitions, she became a schoolteacher in Nottingham and later a governess in Derby.

All this time she was pursuing her writing career, and eventually a serial of hers was published in a popular magazine of the day, *Good Words,* edited by Dr Norman Macleod, and she became one of his regular contributors. Her real breakthrough came in 1871 when her *Tales of the North Riding* appeared, and she could now embark on a full-time writing career, though often supported by the encouragement and material help of her friends.

Thirteen years later *Between the Heather and the Northern Sea* appeared. It was a tale admired by the Victorian politician Gladstone and other well-known people of the day for it gave — and still gives — a genuine picture of life in old Whitby. The description in the novel of a sea rescue was based on an actual event on the 19th January 1881 when Larry Freeman, coxswain of the Whitby-based lifeboat, received a message from the Vicar of Robin Hood's Bay about a vessel in distress. In spite of terrible snowstorms and drifts eight feet high in places the lifeboat was carried overland from Whitby to the bay, a journey of around five miles, by twelve horses and one hundred men. On the first launching the oars broke. Another attempt was made, and finally the shipwrecked crew were rescued.

In chapters fourteen and fifteen of the novel, Mary Linskill gives her account of the rescue. The scene is a place called Soulsgrif Bight:

'Down at the bottom of the narrow rock-like road a dozen or more of the fisher-folk of the place had gathered — it did not seem strange; nothing was more strange save the awful booming of the sea all along the foot of the cliffs...the mad bursting and tossing of the waves that stretched in broken height and shadowy depths across the Bight from Briscoe Point to Soulsgrif Mere...'

One of the bystanders was Ailsie Drew, whose son was on board the schooner Viking that was drifting past Briscoe Point. A horseman arrived and asked about the nearest lifeboat, but was quickly told that it was at Swarthcliff Bay, 'six miles to the south side'. The horseman rode away and eventually someone cried: 'It's the lifeboat!'

The lifeboat had been brought overland on the decision of its captain, who would not risk launching the boat to try and get round Briscoe Point, almost certainly risking the lives of thirty men. As he pointed out to the horsemen:

'She would never get round the Point. But if it were possible to get her overland through the snow she might be launched in the Bight.'

Mary Linskill concludes:

'It was done...and the day and deed will ever live, as brave deeds have lived in England always...'

Her second novel *The Haven Under the Hill,* appearing three years later, gives a picture of the jet-working times — jet being a very hard and shiny variety of the rock lignite. During the last century dozens of workers were engaged in the profitable business of making hand-carved jet jewellery, bric-a-brac and even small tables. (Whitby's Pannett Park Museum has displays of some of the intricately carved pieces.) After the death of the Prince Consort, Queen Victoria set the fashion for jet jewellery. This brought great prosperity to Whitby as the substance is found in abundance in the area. Later, however, imports of cheap jet destroyed the industry, though today it is recovering a little.

The Haven under the Hill gives an insight into the lives of the jet-workers, notably John Gower, master craftsman, his strictly religious wife and their young daughter Dorigen. She is often in trouble for wasting her time reading, instead of doing 'something more useful'. One Sunday, John and his daughter set out to attend service at St Mary's Church on East Cliff near the abbey ruins:

'Everywhere in Kirkgate, from the dockyard at the bottom to the widening harbour-mouth at the top you were reminded of the fact that it ran parallel to the river. They came to the foot of the church steps presently, the ''church stairs'' as people called them still.'

A little way up, Dorigen caught a glimpse of the sea — 'the real sea, not the river'.

The rector, the Rev Marcus Kenningham passed the Gowers, spoke to them and noticed the expression on the little girl's face, saying to himself, ' ''That child is born into trouble as the sparks fly upwards'', as he went up the broad pathway that leads to the church door'.

The novel is concerned with some of that trouble and Dorigen's life and experiences. The book was dedicated to John Lupton of

Headingley, Leeds, for 'unfailing kindness and understanding sympathy made available through many years'. He and his wife had been supportive to the woman who was doing her utmost to be successful — both financially as well as artistically — in a hard profession.

She largely succeeded, and was able to move back to Whitby several years before her most famous novels were published. She lived at Spring Bank in the nearby village of Ruswarp, and died there on the 9th April 1891. Literary visitors tracing her life and the background to her books can see the cross marking her grave in Whitby churchyard, not far from the church she described in her novels. These are still worth rediscovering for people who enjoy an authentic recreation of this most picturesque of regions.

A writer who described a different kind of literary landscape in Whitby is Bram Stoker. The author's horrific novel *Dracula* has been the subject of several leaflets, special weekends and walkabouts in Whitby in recent years. Situated partly around East Cliff, chapters six to eight of the book thrill many people who enjoy retracing the steps of Count Dracula and his victims.

The count owes his existence to Dublin-born Abraham (Bram) Stoker (1847-1912), who graduated from Trinity College, Dublin, in 1870 and became an inspector of the Petty Sessions for the Irish Civil Service. He left this position in 1878 to become the general manager of Sir Henry Irving's theatre company at London's Lyceum Theatre. Not all his time was spent in theatrical circles, however, as he also wrote popular mystery novels and supernatural stories. His most successful work was *Dracula,* published in 1897, and has subsequently been dramatised and filmed many times over.

The chapters based in Whitby are the outcome of his knowledge and love of the old seaport. He first visited it in 1885, and this initial visit was followed by others until 1890. (He also visited more remote Ravenscar to the south of Robin Hood's Bay.) He knew Whitby well, and many of the haunts of the characters in the book can be traced quite easily. A victorian-style memorial seat in his honour was placed at the south end of Spion Kop on West Cliff in April 1980, erected

Mary Linskill.

Bram Stoker.

jointly by the local council and the Dracula Society. From the seat there are fine views across the harbour towards East Cliff and many of the count's haunts.

It will be recalled that the young solicitor Jonathan Harker has journeyed to Transylvania to visit the mysterious Count Dracula who wishes to buy some property in England. Jonathan soon makes the horrible discovery that the count is a vampire — one of the 'un-dead' — but he cannot prevent him, hidden in a box of earth, being brought to Whitby by boat where he escapes.

Two young ladies — Mina, Jonathan's future bride, and her friend Lucy Westenra — are spending their summer holidays staying at a house on East Crescent on West Cliff when they encounter Dracula without realising his identity. One night Mina discovers that Lucy is missing and sets out in search of her, going along North Terrace by the Royal Hotel. Here she stops to gaze across onto moonlit East Cliff and the old church with its surrounding graveyard. There appears to be a white figure with something dark bending over it, and Mina decides it must be Lucy. She descends the drawbridge along Bridge Street, and discovers Lucy asleep on their favourite seat overlooking the sea. The dark figure has disappeared — for the time being. Other episodes relate how Dracula could turn himself into a dog or wolf, and land in such a guise from the sea. Even today the area round the old abbey ruins, the church and the cliffs make such supernatural visitations credible, especially at dusk.

Whitby's most famous twentieth century author is of course Storm Jameson (1891-1987), whose ancestors had lived in the area for over six hundred years. Her father was a sea captain, and her mother was a member of a well-known and old-established family shipping firm. Storm Jameson spent her early childhood at 5 Park Terrace, North Bank, before the family moved to a new house on West Cliff. She had two sisters and a brother who was later killed in World War I, and whose memorial tablet is in St Mary's Church gallery. After attending a local school, followed by Scarborough Municipal School where she was awarded one of the three North Riding scholarships to Leeds University, she gained a first class honours in English literature and language. This was followed by a one year research scholarship to University College, London, from where she transferred herself to King's College. Later she became a copywriter with an advertising agency before embarking on a full-time writing career.

Her autobiography *Journey From the North* (1969) gives an interesting account of her life, authorship and experiences. It provides an illuminating picture of her native town, as well as her keen interest in, and work for, international literature and affairs. She wrote forty-five books — novels, essays, short stories and criticism — between 1919 and 1979, as well as her lengthy autobiography. Some of these were written in London, some in other parts of the country where she lived, such as Bradford and Ilkley. The latter was her home when her husband Guy Chapman was based at Leeds University, and after her morning stint of writing she loved to take long walks over the moors, though she tended to regard the Ilkley moors as being much wilder than those of her native North Riding.

Whitby provided her with the model for Danesacre, a town she records in several of her books. She often returned home to visit her family, and also lived for a time at Ruswarp. From 1929 she occupied a house that overlooked the fields and moors not far from Whitby, where she wrote her novel *A Day Off* (1933). Although many of her novels are on worldwide subjects — during World War II she was president of the international writer's association PEN and helped persecuted poets and writers to escape from Germany — her Yorkshire books, and especially those based on the life of the port, give a good impression of Whitby at the turn of the century. *The Pot Boils and the Scum Rises* was published in 1919, followed in 1927 by *The Lovely Ship*. She started the series with the aim of telling the story of Mary Hansyke, later Mary Harvey, from her birth in 1841 to her death in 1923. She based this on the life of her own grandmother, who had descended from a long line of shipbuilders and had taken over the business herself, guiding it through the days of sail before selling 'at the height of the boom in shipping'. Storm Jameson commented: 'That was something I knew about.'

In another of her novels, *Company Parade* (1934), she gives an account of how one of the characters Russell Harvey and her mother attend the 1921 Armistice Day service at St Mary's Church, and describes the view from the church door overlooking the harbour, the hills around it and the sea. The final paragraph of this novel tells how the main character comes to a turn in the road above Danesacre and sees the town where she was born, the beauty of which has captured so many hearts since Storm Jameson wrote her description and, as we have seen, the imagination of many writers before her.

The Dales and Craven

The Yorkshire Dales offer the visitor some of the most memorable scenery in the country, with its picturesque valleys beginning in the high Pennine moorlands and running east and south into the lowlands of the Vale of York. Literary explorers also have much to interest them, since the Dales have been enjoyed by many writers, the majority of whom did not visit only one place; so it is easiest in this section of our literary survey to take a chronological look at the region.

Two of the earliest literary figures to return time and again to the Dales and celebrate the region in their writing were the Wordsworths, William (1770-1850) and Dorothy (1771-1855). Their love of this part of Yorkshire was fostered at an early age. Just before her death in 1778, Ann Wordsworth had asked her friend and second cousin Elizabeth Threlkeld, who lived in Halifax, to look after her daughter Dorothy instead of the girl remaining with her grandparents, the Cooksons of Penrith. Though both Dorothy and William were born in Cockermouth (now in Cumbria), they visited their maternal grand-parents and stayed with them for a time while they attended school in the town. However, the Wordsworths were never very happy when staying or living with their relations.

Elizabeth Threlkeld did as Ann requested. In 1778 Dorothy joined the other children to whom Miss Threlkeld acted as guardian. She went to live at Halifax and enjoyed a very happy childhood. At first she was a boarder at a school in Hipperholme, but after her father's death in 1783 family finances forced her to move to a cheaper school in Halifax itself. She also took part in the activities of Northgate End Chapel which the Threlkeld family attended. Its members were keenly interested in other subjects besides religion, and here Dorothy developed a keen appreciation of literature and the like, enabling her to become a congenial companion to William.

Dorothy returned to Penrith in the summer of 1787 to spend a holiday there with her brother. They renewed their friendship with Mary Hutchinson and her younger brother Thomas, whom they knew from their schooldays here. Like the Wordsworths, the Hutchinsons were also orphans, and were living with their aunt in Penrith.

In 1799 Dorothy and William returned from a tour of Germany with their friend Samuel Taylor Coleridge. (The two poets had published *Lyrical Ballads* the year before.) Together they all stayed at the Hutchinsons' new home at Sockburn near Northallerton, described by Dorothy as 'a pleasant farm on the banks of the Tees'.

Their journey was by way of Barnard Castle and Richmond. They noticed the fine castle and Grey Friars Tower near where Richmond's theatre had been recently opened in 1788. For many years this theatre was visited by the famous actors and actresses of the day, but eventually it was closed. For a time the building was used for all kinds of untheatrical purposes, but was renovated and reopened as a theatre in 1962. Returning to the Wordsworths, they travelled towards Askrigg, and after spending the night there went on to Hawes, mainly to view the imposing Hardraw Force.

Three years later they were again in Yorkshire. William had at last made up his mind to marry Mary Hutchinson. In July 1802 William and Dorothy set off from Grasmere to visit Mary at Hackness, west of Scarborough, presumably to make arrangements for the wedding. They travelled by carriage as far as Thirsk and then decided to walk the remainder of the way, climbing the very steep Sutton Bank. In her *Journal* Dorothy writes:

'Arrived very hungry [after journeying from Sutton Bank] at Rievaulx. Nothing to eat at the Millers, as we expected, but at an exquisitely neat farmhouse we got some boiled milk and bread. This strengthened us, and I went to look at the ruins — thrushes were singing, cattle feeding among green-grown hillocks about the ruins. These hillocks were scattered over with grovelets of wild roses and other shrubs and covered with wild flowers. I could have stayed in this solemn, quiet spot till evening without a thought of moving but William was waiting for me, in a quarter of an hour I went away.'

Reaching Helmsley, they stayed overnight. Dorothy recorded:

'We reached Helmsley just at dusk. We had a beautiful view of the Castle from the top of the hill. Slept at a very nice Inn (the Old Manor House) and were well treated — bright bellows and floors as smooth as ice. On Friday morning the 15th July we walked to Kirby. Met people coming to Helmsley fair…'

The Old Manor House was next door to the Black Swan Inn in the market place, and is now part of the premises. As they approached the inn on their return journey, Dorothy wrote:

'My heart danced at the sight of its clean outside, bright yellow walls, casements overshadowed with jasmine and its low double gavel-ended front…'

Again the Wordsworths remembered the Black Swan when they came to Yorkshire for William's wedding. This took place at the little church of Brompton-by-Sawdon, south-west of Scarborough, on the 4th October 1802. (Mary Hutchinson was living at her uncle's farm, Gallows Hill, close by.) After the wedding they came to the comfortable little inn once more. Dorothy and Mary admired the castle ruins; then, leaving the bride seated by the fire, William and Dorothy went for a long walk.

William Wordsworth was one of the first sightseers to discover Helmsley as an ideal centre for exploration, and did much to popularise the area. Thirty-six years later the Black Swan became the town's principal coaching inn when a stage coach service began from Leeds through York to Helmsley, and later on to Kirbymoorside.

Dorothy, William and Mary had decided on a short tour of the Dales before the newlyweds returned to Dove Cottage, their Grasmere home. They visited the lovely little town of Wensley and its fine church, and then went on to see nearby Bolton Castle where Mary, Queen of Scots had once been imprisoned in the custody of Lord Scrope. This stongly-built landmark now towers over the tiny village known as Castle Bolton. At one time, agricultural labourers and their families lived in parts of the castle, and in more recent times people have been able to explore parts of it. At the time of writing the castle is being turned into a place that will give visitors some idea of

The Black Swan in Helmsley.

A silhouette of the young Dorothy Wordsworth, the only known likeness.

The RSC's David Delves as Wackford Squeers examining the pump outside
Dotheboys Hall in 1987.

what life and work was like when it was a lived-in part of Wensleydale. The owner, Harry Orde-Powlett, son of Lord Bolton, has planned the transformation based on genuine local knowledge and a love of the dale.

Apart from the castle itself there was not much for the Wordsworths to see, so next they went on to Aysgarth Falls. From there they journeyed to Middleham Castle, the former home of the Nevilles and Richard III. (Despite Shakespeare's portrayal of him, the king is still well-remembered in his own part of Yorkshire, and there is a Richard III Society in his honour.) One of the places that impressed Dorothy most of all was Rievaulx Abbey. It is still possible, especially out of season, to recapture some of the tranquility she must have savoured in the venerable old abbey.

It may be hard to believe that the peaceful riverside setting of the town of Knaresborough was once the scene of a hideous murder, which provided Edward Bulwer-Lytton (1803-1873) with the plot for his novel *Eugene Aram* (1832) and Thomas Hood with the inspiration for his poem *The Dream of Eugene Aram*. In 1744 this Ramsgill-born, Middlemoor man murdered Daniel Clarke and buried his body in St Robert's Cave near the river.

This is not far from the chapel that Celia Fiennes so admired. She was impressed with Knaresborough as a whole, calling it 'a pretty stone built town with a large Market Place'. She was not too impressed, however, with the colour of the River Nidd:

'...the water looks black, I fancy it runs off from the Iron and Sulphur Mines which changes the colour...'

One version of the murder story is that Eugene Aram was in financial difficulties, and together with a flax-worker called Houseman, he joined with Clarke to raise some money. Clarke borrowed various valuable objects from friends on the pretext that he was due a legacy and would return them when it arrived. Meanwhile he intended to pawn the objects, or raise money on them in some other way, but instead sold them outright. Whether or not a disagreement arose about the division of the proceeds, the two quarrelled and Clarke was murdered.

Aram buried Clarke in St Robert's Cave, where the body remained undisturbed for fourteen years. Aram and his wife moved to King's Lynn in Norfolk, where he was well-liked and respected as a teacher. According to one version, some workmen discovered Clarke's body while carrying out excavations. Enquiries were made, Houseman turned king's evidence and the crime was traced to Aram. Thomas Hood's poem gives a slightly different story, for he believed that Aram had foolishly told one of his pupils of the crime. The result:

'Two stern faced men set out from Lynn
Through cold and heavy mist;
And Eugene Aram walked between
With gyves [handcuffs] on his wrist.'

In reality Aram was tried at York, imprisoned in the castle and executed. There is, however, nothing to indicate that such a grim event ever took place as one strolls the path from Knaresborough's Low Bridge towards St Robert's Cave and St Robert's Chapel.

It is easy to trace a well-known literary landscape in the area around Bowes and neighbouring Barnard Castle. Charles Dickens (1812-1870), already a successful journalist, editor and novelist, delighted in campaigning for the less fortunate members of society, especially if his campaign could be backed up with an interesting story. Hearing about the terrible conditions in Yorkshire boarding schools, Dickens set out to research the background which he could use as the basis of his new novel *Nicholas Nickleby* (1838-9). At these badly-run establishments, unwanted boys were boarded for very small fees and with few holidays. Dickens's ally was Charles Smithson of Malton, whose home Easthorpe Hall the novelist often visited. It was Smithson who arranged for the author to be supplied with introductions to a lawyer in Barnard Castle.

So the twenty-six year old Dickens and his illustrator 'Phiz' (H K Browne) travelled north to discover for themselves the truth about these notorious schools. In January 1838, after a long coach journey from London in terrible weather, they arrived at the George Inn in Greta Bridge. Dickens thought of himself as something of a connoisseur of hotels and inns and their settings, and he was not at all impressed with the locality of the George Inn. He described it as 'a bare place with a house standing alone in the midst of a dreary moor'. At the time of Dickens's visit there are thought to have been two other hotels in Greta Bridge, the New Inn and the Morritt Arms.

In *Nicholas Nickleby,* Dickens informs readers:

'The day dragged uncomfortably enough. At about six o'clock that night he [Nicholas] and Mr Squeers, and the little boys, and their united luggage, were all put down together at the George and New Inn, Greta Bridge.'

The next chapter tells how Mr Squeers left Nicholas and the boys:

'...standing with the baggage in the road, to amuse themselves by looking at the coach as it changed horses, while he ran into the tavern and went through the leg-stretching process at the bar. After some minutes he returned with his legs thoroughly stretched, if the hue of his nose, and a short hiccup afforded any criterion; and at the same time there came out of the yard a rusting pony-chaise and a cart, driven by two labouring men.'

From Greta Bridge, Dickens and Phiz set off for neighouring Barnard Castle and Bowes. They called on Mr R Barnes, a lawyer of the former town, but he was away from home, so Dickens left the introductory letter from his friend Smithson and went on to wait at the King's Head Hotel. According to the author's preface, Mr Barnes:

'...came down at night, through the snow, to the inn where I was staying...I recollect that he was a jovial, ruddy broad-faced man; that we got acquainted directly; and that we talked about all kinds of subjects, except the schools, which he showed a great anxiety to avoid'.

After the lawyer had refreshed himself with some wine, he advised Dickens not to allow his widowed friend to send her son to one of these schools. (Dickens had invented this lady as an excuse for his enquiries.) He said that the young boy would be better off turned out into the world to make his own way than to be sent to one of them. Dickens added in his preface, 'I sometimes imagine that I descry a faint reflection of him [the lawyer] in John Broadie', this being the man who helps Nicholas and Smike to escape from Dotheboys Hall.

Although Barnard Castle is in the neighbouring county of Durham, it is necessary to visit it in order to follow through the whole of Dickens' investigative search. He and Phiz found the King's Head a pleasant hotel, much more to their liking. In *Nicholas Nickleby*, Newman Noggs, Ralph Nickleby's downtrodden clerk, advises Nicholas to call at this hotel, where there is 'good ale' and if he mentions his name he will not be charged for it, for he was once well-known there from the time when he was 'a gentleman'.

Further enquiries took place in the little town, one of them at Master Humphrey's shop where Dickens sought the opinion of its owner about the state of the local schools. Today a tablet marks the site of this small shop, not far from the parish church. Its name is immortalised in Dickens's periodical *Master Humphrey's Clock,* begun in 1840.

The author and illustrator travelled next to Bowes, where they stayed at the Unicorn Inn. The original stone-built Dotheboys Hall still exists here, though now it has been converted into private dwellings. It stands towards one end of the village, bordering the road. This was the Academy of Mr William Shaw which Dickens saw in 1838. Here boys experienced the horrors that were later carried out at the fictitious school where Nicholas became usher. Six years before Dickens's visit, Mr Shaw had been convicted of neglecting his pupils, and on opening his door to the two strange callers, he was so suspicious that he refused to admit them. But with his other investigations, the astute author learned enough for his purpose.

Soon after the publication of Dickens's novel, Mr Shaw's Academy ceased to exist. Today the exterior of the building tallies with the description given in the novel, though naturally there have been alterations over the intervening years. On their arrival in Greta Bridge, when Nicholas asks how far it still is to Dotheboys Hall, Squeers advises him that:

'You needn't call it a Hall down here...We call it a Hall up in London, because it sounds better, but they don't know it by that name in these parts.'

Nicholas's first impressions of the 'Hall' only serve to reinforce this:

'…the school was a long, cold-looking house, one story high, with a few straggling outbuildings behind, and a barn and stable adjoining.'

The original pump under which Mr Wackford Squeers's pupils had to wash in all weathers remains, though in the nineteenth century this practise might not have been regarded as of as much of a hardship in the Dales as it undoubtedly would have been in more southern counties.

In 1987, when the Royal Shakespeare Company's world-renowned production of *Nicholas Nickleby* was staged at Newcastle's Theatre Royal, a group of actors and actresses visited Bowes to see the background that Dickens had used for his book. David Delves, who was playing the part of Squeers, had his photograph taken in costume examining the pump under which the fictional character forced his charges to wash.

Other visitors intent on discovering the background for Dickens's novel should take a stroll round Bowes churchyard, not far from the castle. It contains a memorial to Smike, the unfortunate feeble-minded boy who made such a hero of Nicholas. In reality the grave is that of George Ashton Taylor of Trowbridge, Wiltshire, who died suddenly aged nineteen at Mr Shaw's Academy on the 13th April 1822. Dickens wrote of his discovery of the grave:

'The first gravestone I stumbled on that dreary afternoon was over a boy who had died suddenly. I suppose his heart broke. He died in this wretched place, and I think his ghost put Smike into my mind on the spot.'

Charles Dickens often visited other parts of Yorkshire, mostly while giving public readings of his novels, though his opinions of the towns and cities he saw on these occasions seem slightly coloured by the reception given to his performances!

From Bowes it is easy to trace the background of another Victorian author whose childhood was partly spent in this most northern part of Yorkshire. In 1843 Sir Robert Peel had approached the Rev Charles Dodgson of Daresbury, Cheshire with the offer of the living of Croft, not far from historic Richmond. He accepted the offer, even though it was an upheaval to move a large family across England. For his son, twelve year old Charles Lutwidge Dodgson (1832-1898), it was the beginning of a new life, one in which he would have closer contact with people beyond his family circle. Also for the first time he would attend school, as a boarder, for until then he had been taught by his father at home.

The school was Richmond Grammar School which had gained a good reputation under James Tate, one continued by his son — also named James Tate — who became Charles's first headmaster. The young pupil was to live in what is now Swale House along Frenchgate, and visitors can see the house where he stayed from 1844 until 1846. An inscription reads:

> 'Great Channel
> affectionately known as
> 'Cloaca Maxima'
> when Swale House was
> the residence of James Tate
> and of his son and namesake,
> Masters of Richmond School
> 1796-1833 and 1833 respectively.
> Scholars who boarded with them here
> included Lewis Carroll, the boy poet Herbert Knowles
> and two sons of Earl Grey, Prime Minister 1833-1838.'

Herbert Knowles was a West Riding boy, born in the Huddersfield area, whom we shall meet again in the appropriate chapter. Lewis Carroll was, of course, the pseudonym of Charles L Dodgson in later life, when he discovered a second career as the author of such books as *Alice's Adventures in Wonderland.*

His first day at school was the 1st August 1844, and nine days later his parents visited Richmond to see how he liked his new environment. Already his two eldest sisters Frances and Elizabeth had received a letter telling something of his fellow pupils, and the tricks they had attempted to play on the new boy until they tired of it.

Football, wrestling, leapfrog and fighting are listed as the school sports. Young Charles proved himself an ideal pupil and his headmaster soon discovered that the boy from Croft Rectory was one with unusual talents. At the end of June 1845, Mr Tate sent a report to Charles's parents stating:

'Sufficient opportunities have been allowed to draw from actual observation an estimate of your son's character and abilities. I do not hesitate to express my opinion that he possesses, along with other and natural endowments, a very uncommon share of genius. Gentle and cheerful in his intercourse with others, playful and ready in conversation, he has acquirements and knowledge far beyond his years; so jealous of error, that he will not rest satisfied without a most exact solution of whatever appears to him obscure.'

Such a good headmaster as Mr Tate well knew that parents could be so flattered by such complimentary words about their offspring that they might pass it on to the child concerned. In Victorian times encouragement was allowed, but not too much praise, so he penned the condition:

'You must not entrust your son with full knowledge of his superiority over other boys.'

Here was something for the young boy to live up to!

One of Charles's early poems was published in the school magazine, and this fostered his love of writing. Already he was in the habit of making up stories, poems, puzzles and games for the younger members of his family.

Early in 1846 his father moved him from Richmond School and sent him to Rugby School. At the time, the headmaster of this public school — made famous by Dr Arnold — was Dr A C Tait, who later became the Archbishop of Canterbury. On leaving Richmond School, his former headmaster assured Charles's parents:

'I shall always feel a particular interest in the gentle, intelligent and well-educated boy who is now leaving us.'

Charles himself must have thought a great deal about his first headmaster, for he continued to keep in touch with him during his holidays at Croft. At the rectory he continued to entertain his brothers and sisters. He produced a home-made magazine, written and edited by himself, carrying the rather daunting title of *Useful and Instructive Poetry,* which ran for six months. Another, *The Rectory Umbrella,* had in one issue a tale with the intriguing title of *A Walking Stick of Destiny.* Even on vacations from Christ Church, Oxford, he continued to write light verse parodies and serial stories, and some of this early work was published in the *Whitby Gazette Summer Supplement* of 1854, though not under his own name.

Charles Dodgson became a clergyman in 1861, though never a fully-ordained priest, and remained a deacon all his life. His career was in the field of mathematics, and he was appointed lecturer in mathematics at his old Oxford college in 1855. A second career opened up to him, however, when on a river boat trip in 1865 he told the story of Alice, the White Rabbit and the Queen of Hearts to Alice, Edith and Lorina Liddle, the daughters of the Dean of Christ Church, and published it as *Alice's Adventures in Wonderland.* Lewis Carroll, as he made himself known to his reading public, followed this up with *Through the Looking Glass and What Alice Found There* (1871), *The Hunting of the Snark* (1876) and *Sylvie and Bruno* (1889).

Visitors tracing Lewis Carroll's early life in Croft can see the memorial window to him in the small church of St Peter where his father was rector. (He also served as Archdeacon of Cleveland and a canon of Ripon Cathedral.) Both his parents are buried in the churchyard of this picturesque village.

Another clergyman-turned-author who helped to make part of the Dales and Craven better-known to the general public was the Rev Charles Kingsley (1819-1875). Born at Holme in Devonshire, he went to King's College, London, and studied classics at Magdalene College, Cambridge, before becoming Rector of Eversley in Hampshire. In these early years he visited Coverdale, an offshoot of Wensleydale, in May 1845. Being a learned cleric he would have no doubt recollected that Miles Coverdale (1488-1568), the translator of the Bible, had been born in this remote dale. (His version of the psalms are still contained in the 1662 Prayer Book.) Kingsley may well have been more impressed with the scenery, however, for he was a

The exterior of Croft Church. Lewis Carroll's parents are buried in the churchyard.

LEWIS CARROLL
1832-1898

WAS THE ELDEST SON OF
THE VENERABLE CHARLES DODGSON
RECTOR OF CROFT
AND ARCHDEACON OF RICHMOND
1843-1868

HE SPENT HIS BOYHOOD YEARS
AT CROFT RECTORY WHERE SOME
OF HIS EARLY WRITINGS WERE DONE
FROM A PLAYFUL INVERSION
OF HIS BAPTISMAL NAMES
CHARLES LUTWIDGE
HE FORMED THE PEN NAME
BY WHICH MILLIONS OF CHILDREN
WHO LOVE HIS WORKS
HAVE COME TO KNOW HIM

LESS WIDELY KNOWN
FROM THAT SAME HAND
COME THESE NOSTALGIC LINES

I'd give all wealth that years have piled,
the slow result of life's decay,
To be once more a little child
for one bright summer day.

The memorial tablet to Lewis Carroll at Croft Church.

countryman at heart. He also visited Jervaulx Abbey — between Middleham and Masham — where he chose two plants to send back to his wife, Fanny, explaining that:

'...the forget-me-not was from the ruined High Altar, the saxifrage from the Refectory'.

At this time, Kingsley had recently been appointed Canon of Middleham by Dean Wood, though this involved no duties and no financial reward, merely the title. He was therefore staying in the area before being installed into this position at Middleham Church. The local landowner was a Mr Topham, about whom Kingsley wrote:

'The greatest worthy I have for some time seen, a perfect specimen of an unsophisticated Yorkshire squire.'

Another thing that impressed him was 'everybody's kindness here — the mere meeting one is sufficient to cause an invitation to stay'. Evidence of this is shown by the fact that people were willing to lend Kingsley — a keen fisherman — enough tackle for him to pursue his hobby.

Kingsley's best-known literary links are, however, with the area around Malham and Arncliffe. In 1858 he spent a holiday in Yorkshire with W E Forster, the Bradford Quaker who did much for education, and who had offered to show him round the places connected with the rising of the north in 1569. Together they travelled through Wharfedale, Skipton, Dent and Ripon, visiting most of the ruined Yorkshire abbeys on their way. From the ancient city of Ripon they journeyed on to Malham to stay with Walter Morrison, the wealthy landowner there. He lived at Tarn House, which is now the Malham Tarn Field Centre, situated in the midst of a superb nature reserve. Apart from being a country landower, he was also a benefactor of much of Craven; he was a patron of Giggleswick School, and erected a chapel there to mark Queen Victoria's Diamond Jubilee. Kingsley's ultimate aim was to write a historical novel about the rising of the north, so he collected as much background information as possible. His enthusiasm rose, and he observed that:

'...the book grows on me. I see my way as clear as day. How I will write when I get home...'

Whatever his hopes, the novel was never written. Instead out of his sightseeing in the Malham area came the children's classic *The Water Babies* (1863). The plight of little chimney-sweeps was one that Kingsley had absorbed into his social conscience, especially as Lord Shaftesbury, the great reformer against child labour, had recently worked on a report about the subject. This included horrific details of how boys of six years old were regarded as being of 'a nice trainable age' for clambering up chimneys to help clear them of soot.

Kingsley was a great believer in the theory that if people wished to understand history they should first try to understand men and women. Like his contemporary, the critic and philospher Thomas Carlyle, he advised the study of history through biographies. One outcome of his theory is the books he wrote for his own children. *Heroes* (1856) had been dedicated to 'Rose, Maurice and Mary'. He described the work as 'a little present of old Greek fairy tales', but, in typically Victorian manner, he could not help including a moral in his introduction: 'Do right and God will help you.'

Strong-minded Mrs Kingsley reminded him a few years later that as he had written a book for his other children, he ought to write one for 'Baby', his youngest son Grenville. Like the obedient husband he was, Charles is reputed to have gone into his study and returned only half an hour later with the first chapter of *The Water Babies*. It soon proved to be a firm favourite with the Macmillan children, who were staying with the Kingsley's at Eversley Rectory in 1863.

It is widely thought that the original inspiration for the story of Tom, the young chimney-sweep employed by the evil Mr Grimes, and his adventures as a 'water baby', came to Kingsley while visiting Malham Tarn several years previously. The book states:

'A mile off and a thousand feet down Tom found the Tarn, though it seemed as if he could have chucked a pebble on to the back of the woman in the red petticoat who was weeding in her cottage garden.'

Later Kingsley tells how Tom glanced through the open rose-covered doorway into the cottage and saw the red-petticoated lady once again. In reality the model for this woman was a Miss Henderson, who lived at Bridge End, Arncliffe. Kingsley knew the cottage well, as he had often walked in the area and had once enjoyed tea with her.

The bells that Tom heard as he came down the little river are said to have been those of St Michael's Church at Kirby Malham, a mile from Malham village. Inside the church, the chancel commemorates the lives and achievements of many well-known local people, including Kingsley's friend Walter Morrison. When visitors such as Kingsley were staying at his home, Tarn House, he loved nothing better than to take them sightseeing to Yorkshire's beauty spots, or perhaps a trip into Settle on market days to meet the local farmers. On one such visit, Kingsley described how he had been impressed with the view from Ingleborough with 'the whole world to the west, the Lake District and the western sea beyond Lancaster'. He had heard of the grandeur of Gordale, and discovered for himself that the reports had not exaggerated.

Kingsley was probably aware of the poet Thomas Gray's impressions written to a friend after a visit to Malham in 1769. The poet had arrived in the village from Settle by coach. He described it as being 'in the bosom of mountains, seated in a wild and dreary valley'. He went on to discover that:

'...the hills opened again into a large space and then further away is barred by a stream that at the height of fifty feet gushed from a leak in the rock, and spreading in large sheets on its broken front, dashes from steep to steep and then rattles away in a torrent down the valley.'

Though he was greatly impressed with the beauty of the Dales, nervously-constituted Gray was rather intimidated when his explorations took him to Gordale Scar. He watched in amazement as:

'...on the cliffs above were a few goats, one of them danced and scratched an ear with its hind foot in a place where I would not have stood still for all the world.'

Another poet who dearly loved the Dales, especially the largest, Wensleydale, was Sir William Watson (1858-1935). He was born in Peel Place, Burley-in-Wharfedale, where his father John William Watson had a twine business. When the younger William was only three years old, the business was sold and the family moved to the

Liverpool area. However, visits to Yorkshire, and especially Wensley-dale, were frequent.

His mother was a Wensleydale woman whose father had been a stocking dealer at Askrigg (William's first visit to Askrigg was not until 1898), but it was from his father that he really inherited his love of the Yorkshire Dales. As he grew older, William discovered that some of his maternal ancestors had deep-rooted links in the Dales, and one was buried in Richmond churchyard. He then set about tracing his forebears long before the subject was the popular pursuit it is today. He succeeded in going as far back as the fourteenth century and discovered that one ancestor was connected with Middleham Castle.

From an early age he had been interested in poetry, and he was reputed to have been able to recite the whole of *Paradise Lost* when he was only nine years old — though whether he understood much of it is another matter! Before long he began to write verse of his own, and, like many poets, he paid for the publication of his first book of poetry. Yet he was determined to make his living by writing. Many of his poems have a sombre tone, such as *Wordsworth's Grave* (1890), *The Tomb of Burns* — both written from his personal impression of their burial places — and *Lachrymae Musarum* (1892), mourning Tenyson's death.

He hoped one day to become Poet Laureate, but was never chosen. But throughout his career he maintained his love of the Dales. On one occasion he wrote, 'I should like to have my connection with these grand parts of England better known.' His wish has been partly granted as today one of his best-loved poems celebrates Wensleydale's only lake, Semerwater. Halliwell Sutcliffe, who will be mentioned later in this chapter, said of this poem that 'Semerwater is the most alluring ballad of our modern times.'

A literary traveller whose views on York we have already read is Nathaniel Hawthorne, but he and his family also visited Craven and were most impressed by it. On the 10th April 1857, the writer, his wife and son Julian came to Skipton:

'Skipton is an ancient town and has an ancient though thoroughly repaired aspect — the site is irregular and rising gradually towards Skipton Castle which overlooks the town.'

Such an inquisitive sightseer as Hawthorne would no doubt have learned that the castle's most indomitable occupant was undoubtedly Lady Anne Clifford, born there in 1590. She rebuilt much of the castle after the Civil War, and planted the yew tree in Conduit Court to celebrate its restoration in 1659. Her tutor from her early years until her marriage in 1609 was the poet Samuel Daniel (1563-1619), who also had a growing career at the time as a court poet to James I, and wrote many masques for the king. These were dramatic spectacles, involving much music and costume, performed at court, and Lady Anne acted in several of these written by her tutor. Daniel was admired by many of his contemporaries, though Ben Jonson called him 'a good honest man...but no poet'.

At the time of Hawthorne's visit, this ancient stronghold of the Cliffords belonged to Sir Richard Tufton, but the novelist and his family were shown round by his housekeeper. Hawthorne described the rooms as:

'...rather sombre and gloomy — not the less so for what has been done to modernise them, for instance, modern paper hangings and in some of the rooms, marble fireplaces. Tapestry needed but that hanging is "ghastly" and representing persons being tortured.'

He decided that 'the castle is not at all crumbly, but in excellent repair though so venerable'.

It was not so much the venerable Bolton Priory that impressed him and his family when they travelled to see this monastic ruin on the next day, Easter Sunday, but the beauty of its situation:

'...the ruin of the Priory is at the bottom of the beautiful valley about a quarter of a mile off, and well as the monks knew how to choose the site of their establishments I think they never chose a better site than this — in the green lap of protecting hills, besides a stream and with peace and fertility looking down upon it on every side.'

Hawthorne and his family pursued their explorations:

'A few yards from this hunting box [the hunting lodge of the Duke of Devonshire] are the remains of the old Priory, consisting of the nave of the old church, which is still in good repair and used as the worshiping place of the neighbourhood, and the old choir, roofless with broken circles, ivy-grown but not so rich or rare a ruin as either Melrose, Netley or Furness. Its situation makes its charm. It stands near the River Wharfe — a broad and rapid stream...'

From Bolton they journeyed on to York, as is mentioned in the first chapter.

The art critic John Ruskin, who will be discussed more fully in the chapter on South Yorkshire, was a frequent visitor to this part of Yorkshire. He visited Malham, staying at the Buck Inn, and was entertained by Walter Morrison at Malham Tarn House. In *Prospero* he noted of Malham Cove that 'the stones of the brook were softer with moss than any silken pillow'.

His main aim was often to lecture on art or pursue his studies, for example such as that of the scenery that Turner used in his Yorkshire pictures. For this latter purpose he frequently stayed at Farnley Hall near Otley from 1851 onwards, where Turner had been such a welcome guest of Mr Walter Fawkes. Turner often used it as a base for his Yorkshire painting expeditions between 1806 and 1820, and at one time there were no fewer than 170 of the artist's drawings at the hall, though some have since been sold. Ruskin was convinced that the power of the landscape around here had the deepest effect on Turner's art, since he wrote:

'The scenery whose influence I can trace most definitely throughout his [Turner's] works is that of Yorkshire.'

One can still easily trace Ruskin's visits in Yorkshire. He often visited Knaresborough, greatly admiring the little town and on one occasion he stayed in what he described as 'a modern house'. Here he: '...dare not stir a foot for fear of setting one of the modern appliances going and not being able to stop them.'

He did not, however, say what the purpose of these gadgets was! Ruskin was always more at home with genuine craft-made articles rather than mass-produced modern appliances.

From Knaresborough we follow Ruskin north to nearby Ripon, where he stayed for a few days in 1876. During his time here he travelled the two miles to Fountains Abbey, which he enthusiastically described as 'a lovely ruin' and noted:

'Truly nothing like that ever seen by me — showing what St George can do...'

The 'St George' referred to was the Guild of St George, founded by him in Sheffield for the encouragement of true old English crafts-manship. His opinion on the abbey is all the more interesting when one remembers that from an early age Ruskin had visited the continent with his parents, and was accustomed to seeing the fine cities and ancient buildings over there.

His delight in Fountains Abbey is understandable when one considers its site, on the banks of the River Skell as it flows through a secluded valley; and its great antiquity, founded as it was in 1132 by dissident monks from St Mary's Abbey in York. Though the abbey Ruskin admired was, as he said, a ruin, it was still by far the best preserved of the great religious houses that were destroyed after the dissolution of the monasteries in 1538. Ruskin's delight in the abbey has been shared by many other writers, including Ebenezer Elliott of South Yorkshire, Adam Sedgewick of Dent and the novelist Thomas Armstrong, one of its most enthusiastic admirers.

Nearer our own times, the writer Gordon Home described the abbey as:

'...so magnificent and the roofless church is so impressively solemn that, although the place is visited by many thousands each year, yet if you choose a day when the weather or some other circumstances keep other people away, you might easily imagine that you were visiting the park and ruin as a splendid privilege...and not as one of the public who are allowed to come and go with very few restrictions beyond the payment of a shilling.'

Around the same time the well-known Yorkshire topographical writer and artist Edmund Bogg decided:

'To adequately describe this scene, beautiful even today in mid-winter, is almost beyond the power of pen, the history of this romantic wreck being so perfect and lovely.'

Twenty years later H V Morton, during his exploration for his *In Search of...* volumes and *The Call of England,* delighted in the abbeys of Fountains, Jervaulx and Rievaulx, recommending all three:

'I say to any man or woman in England who is looking for a spiritual experience "Go to Ripon and visit these abbeys in turn".'

Today visitors can see something of the mystery and grandeur that has captured so many from past generations, since both the abbey and the deer park of Studley Royal are owned by the National Trust.

Anyone wishing to discover the literary background of Bradford-born William Riley (1866-1961) can do no better than set out to explore the Dales, especially Wharfedale and nearby Craven. Educated at Bradford Grammar School, Riley enjoyed recalling that two of his fellow pupils had been the composer, Frederick Delius, and Cutcliffe Hyne. The latter's father was Vicar of North Bierley Church and the young Cutcliffe is reputed once to have climbed the little bell turret and hung onto the weathervane at the top! In later life, Hyne became better known for his 'Captain Kettle' tales of adventure and *Ben Watson* (1926), his novel set in the Dales. He is buried in Kettlewell Churchyard.

William Riley's first career was with the family firm of 'Riley Brothers, Lantern Slide Manufacturers of Bradford', and he eventually became its managing director. An account of the history of the firm, with some fascinating old pictures of Bradford, is displayed in one of the galleries of the National Museum of Photography in Bradford.

The story of how Grace Holden came to her Yorkshire-born father's home, and her life in the small village of Windyridge and the neighbouring hamlets, was originally told as a kind of serial to some bereaved friends. This was in 1911, long before the days of radio and television which could provide entertainment. Each instalment was written daily and told each evening. On completing the tale, the listeners, who included his wife, insisted that the story should be published. After persuasion, the names of several publishers were placed in a hat and one of the last to go in was that of a new firm, Herbert Jenkins Ltd. That name was the one drawn out.

William Riley prided himself on the fact that he had not asked any feminine advice when it came to writing his novel, even regarding fashion, though he had glanced at one or two ladies' magazines on the

Malham Tarn.

Malham Cove, drawn and etched by William Westall ARA.

Fountains Abbey.

William Riley.

subject. Under sufferance he sent his manuscript to the chosen publishers, and signed his letter 'W Riley'. The reply came addressed to 'Miss W Riley', and when he walked into the publisher's office to keep his appointment to discuss his book the publisher was amazed to see a middle-aged gentleman — since because of the manuscript's subject matter and authentic tone he had expected a young lady!

William Riley's serial for a small group of friends soon found a much larger audience when it was published as the novel *Windyridge*. Shortly afterwards, houses began to spring up all over the land bearing the name of Windyridge. Other books followed, and though all were successful none matched his first novel's record sales.

As a keen walker, Riley explored most of the Dales and was very familiar with them. He moved to Silverdale, Morecambe, in 1919 because of his wife's ill-health, living first in a house he naturally called Windyridge, and then moved further into the village to Yew Tree House. However, he often returned to his native county, sometimes to give lectures, sometimes to preach and take services. He was a long-serving Methodist local preacher with especially strong links with the Shipley circuit.

Of his novels he once told the writer:

'I never construct a plot, just sit down and write in my den and let the story tell itself.'

As it resulted in the portrayal of convincing and believable characters, this method was no doubt best for him. (His 'den' was a second floor study in Yew Tree House.) Most of his novels give a composite picture of a typical Yorkshire village in the late nineteenth and early twentieth centuries, and its inhabitants such as the local squire and the rector or vicar. He often used the towns he knew and loved from his early life as models for his fictional creations, and the keen reader has to use a little literary detective work to work out the real place from its name and description.

The clues are there though: Girston was the upper Dales metropolis and was in reality Grassington; Norton Towers was Barden Towers; Romanton, Ilkley; Netherleigh, Otley, with a Bastion instead of a Chevin; Broadbeck was Bradford and Airlee, Leeds; whilst Windyridge was, of course, Hawksworth.

He had a great ability to give a feeling of what life must have been like for the ordinary people of the time. For example, in *A Window In Craven,* one of the characters is Gideon Capstick, an old stone-waller who was not only expert at his craft but knew how each stone he used came to be suitable for his particular purpose. The reader is told:

'Gideon knew himself to be unsurpassed in his own line, and believed himself to be unsurpassable. To him the business of dry-stone walling was the most important and most exacting of any; to have scamped his work because there was no overseer, because nobody would be any the wiser, would have been sacrilegious — nothing less; not so much an irreverence to his employer, as to the wall itself whose right it was to be soundly built.'

With such descriptions the novel, like many of his others, gives a picture of a way of life that is now disappearing, and sadly until very recently such age-old skills were in great danger of dying out completely.

Only a small proportion of William Riley's characters can be classed as speaking pure dialect, mainly, as he explained, because it is often difficult to read by people not familiar with it. He therefore used a way of spelling that conveyed a dialect meaning without puzzling his non-Yorkshire readers. His work, however, does contain words and sayings peculiar to the county, or one specific area of it. They show the attention to detail that Riley prided himself upon.

In his novel *Rachel Bland's Inheritance,* Riley describes a visit by two of the characters to the ancient parish church of Keepton (Skipton):

'...and the figures in the painted windows looked down upon them as they leaned against the richly carved marble tombs.'

Incidentally a point of interest to modern 'literary detectives' is the Longfellow tombstone now fixed to the west wall of this church's interior. The inscription is in memory of the Longfellow family, one of whom was the uncle of the nineteenth century American poet Henry Wadsworth Longfellow.

Just before he died, William Riley's autobiography, *Sunset Reflections,* was published. At the time when it appeared, he was called the 'ninety-one year old father of Yorkshire novelists', a title his many readers would still approve of.

Another writer of the turn of the century who portrayed the Dales in stories and poetry was Dorothy Una Ratcliffe. Born at the end of the last century — she died in 1967 — she began to write when she was only ten years old, and before long she and her sister had founded a manuscript magazine *Fragments*. Later the title was changed to *Microcosm,* this being taken from Sir Thomas Browne's lines:

'There is no man alone, because every man is a Microcosm and carries the world with him.'

The magazine was published from an office in Leeds, financed mainly by the girls' father George Benson Clough and later by Lord Brotherton, founder of the Brotherton Library at Leeds University. D U R, as she liked to be known, helped to choose volumes for the library and her collection of books on the Romanies is now part of it. The *Microcosm* ran for twenty-five years, raising a considerable amount of money for charity. Dorothy Una Ratcliffe also wrote many fine dialect poems, drama and short stories.

Kirby Malzeard and the moors around it can be classed as her country, as for many years she lived in a house at Leverton and involved herself in the area's day-to-day activities. Many of her 'Mrs Buffey' stories are set in this part of the Dales.

Another facet to her life was the interest she showed in the Romanies. She endeavoured to understand their lives and language, customs and traditions, partly because she was proud of having Romany forebears. Something of this interest is conveyed in *The Cranesbill Caravan,* set in Wensleydale where she and her husband used to stop at a farm. (This was long before the days of purpose-built caravan sites.) It conveys a picture of caravanning in the Dales, and gives an insight into the lives and work of the people of the area, as well as those met on these holidays.

The old city of Ripon with its imposing cathedral has its own literary connection, since the novelist Naomi Jacobs (1889-1964) was born here. The Unicorn Hotel in a corner of the market place was kept by her grandfather, and she related that he made a good success of it. Educated in Middlesbrough, she became an actress and later pursued a career as a writer. Her first novel. *Jacob Ussher,* was published in

1926, and was followed by others such as *Cap of Youth* (1941) and *Private Gollantz* (1943). But it is her series of autobiographical volumes entitled *Me...* that tell of her travels and home in Italy, as well as her love of her native county, and she portrays its people and their lives in some of her lesser-known novels.

About fifteen miles to the north-east of Ripon stand the imposing ruins of Rievaulx Abbey, situated in a deep and narrow valley close to the River Rye and overshadowed by the Hambleton Hills. It was founded in 1131 by the Norman knight Sir Walter D'Espec in order that he might retire to become a Cistercian monk, and he spent the last two years of his life here. As well as the Wordsworths, another writer who knew Rievaulx as a boy and loved it all his life was Sir Herbert Read (1893-1968), remembered chiefly for his poetry and art criticism. He was born at Muscoates Grange near Nunnington, where his family had farmed for over two hundred years. He and a slightly older cousin would set out on excursions to the abbey, often from their aunt's house at nearby Helmsley. He later mentioned how Rievaulx had played an important part in the development of his imaginative powers.

While he was still a boy his father died. The farm had to be sold and he and his brother were sent to a boarding school in Halifax. The industrial landscape must have seemed bleak and grim to someone brought up in sylvan Ryedale. After leaving school he got a job as a clerk in a Leeds bank, but all this time young Herbert was determined to carve out a better career for himself. He gives us something of his ambitions and how he set out to fulfil them in the first volume of his autobiography, *The Innocent Eye* (1933). (Later volumes deal with his adult life.)

He never forgot his old home and the area around Kirbymoorside. He knew the only way to return to his beloved Ryedale was through his own efforts. As he aimed to win a place at Leeds University, this meant study, study and more study, firstly at night school and then at Leeds's public library. One of his night school teachers had a great love of literature, and his infectious enthusiasm for his subject helped young Read to gain some extra confidence in his own writings, especially poetry. He eventually showed some of his earliest efforts to his teacher, and his praise prompted the publication of his first book of verse, at his own expense, in 1915. His literary career continued, though World War I interrupted his studies. He eventually entered the civil service, and one of his later jobs was that of keeper of the Victoria and Albert Museum's section of ceramics — work that fostered his love of art even more.

His *Collected Poems* appeared in 1926, followed by other works including *In Defence of Shelley* (1938), *A Coat of Many Colours,* and his only novel, *The Green Child* (1935), an allegorical fantasy set in the part of Yorkshire he knew and loved. Two lines of his poetry expressed his abiding hope.

'God grant I may return to be
Between the Riccall and the Rye.'

This hope was fulfilled. He returned to live in Stonegrave Old Rectory, only a mile and a half from his boyhood home, in 1949 and continued his writing career. The Old Rectory is a Georgian house built in 1748. According to Sir Herbert's third son, Piers Paul Read, born in 1941 and himself a well-known novelist, his father liked to imagine that two famous clergymen-writers of the past, Laurence Sterne and Sydney Smith, had once visited the Old Rectory and he hoped their spirits still lingered in its passages.

Sir Herbert Read is buried in the rather remote but peaceful churchyard of St Gregory Minster, Kirkdale, a place he knew and loved as a child.

Although Halliwell Sutcliffe (1870-1937) was born in the West Riding, his books cover many parts of Yorkshire, including the Dales. (Novels set in 'Brontëland' will be mentioned in a later chapter.) He was born on the 25th April at the house of a relation in Thackley near Bradford, although his parents' house was at Lee near Haworth where his father John was the local schoolmaster. When his father became headmaster of Bingley Grammar School the family moved to this pleasant little town. Halliwell attended his father's school, and later went up to Cambridge where he obtained a BA degree.

His first career was to follow in his father's footsteps as a teacher, but he soon decided he wanted to become an author. During his life he wrote many novels and topographical works. The latter were based on his own journeys and research, mostly on foot, and include *The Striding Dales*. Similarly, he based his novels on personal observation. These include *A Bachelor in Arcady* (1904) and its sequel *Benedict in Arcady*. Though the books are set in Wharfedale, the actual location for the garden featured in the novels was based on Castlefields House in Crossflatts near Bingley, a later home of his parents. Both are rather romantic novels, depicting the leisurely life of a young man who marries the local squire's daughter. The introduction to the first describes the pattern of the books:

'A little book concerning the whereabouts of Arcady, its denizens, two footed and four footed, with notes as to the folk speech and habits of the same...'

Later he depicts the changing seasons in his 'Arcady':

'It is mid-October now, and winter looks tentatively at us from between the half-naked trees. Why will people assume that when spring has come and gone, when autumn has long since shaken farewell hands with summer, there is nothing to do but wait for another spring? This mid-October period in itself is beautiful beyond belief, up here in these northern lands, where there are hills and moors...'

After his marriage, Halliwell Sutcliffe went to live at White Abbey in lovely Linton-in-Craven, and it is here that he wrote many of his books. He attended worship at the local St Michael and All Angels Church. His funeral service was held at St Wilfred's Church in Burnsall, and his ashes were scattered near Linton. A mark of the respect that this Yorkshire writer inspired is the special exhibition that was held at the Upper Wharfedale Museum at Grassington in 1987 in honour of the fiftieth anniversary of his death.

Thomas Armstrong (1899-1978) was correct when he described his home county as being 'two Yorkshires'. He is one of the authors who have taken settings for their novels from all parts of Yorkshire, so can never truly be classed as 'regional' novelists, since the county from which they draw their inspiration is so large.

Thomas Armstrong was born in Airedale, and educated at Wakefield Grammar School and later Dartmouth Naval College. He served in the Royal Navy during World War I, returning after the war to his family's textile business. While travelling on business he would devote his spare time to writing stories, but without much success, so he decided to devote his time to writing a novel on a subject he knew something about.

After three years of writing and publishers' rejections, *The Crowthers of Bankdam* was accepted in 1940. It soon became a best-seller and was later filmed as *The Master of Bankdam*.

Joshua Crowther, younger son of 'the Master', is delighted when he discovers that Yorkshire does not consist only of gloomy mills and mines, grim villages and dirty towns. There is another Yorkshire, and once he visits the Dales and its ruined abbeys and seen the waterfalls and the sea, he is determined to share his discovery with his family. He tries to convince his sister Mary, but she is not enthralled. However his wife, a former weaver, is much more interested, especially when he takes her to visit this other Yorkshire he has discovered.

One of these expeditions is into Wensleydale, where they visit Bedale, Jervaulx Abbey, Bolton Castle and Fountains Abbey. Joshua Crowther has taken up sketching and has brought all the necessary equipment for his new hobby — which he takes very seriously indeed. He tells his wife that it is the first big job he has tackled, and wishes he could draw better:

'The prospect was indeed lovely — the unutterable peace and quietude of the fragrant Yorkshire countryside, the graceful Perpendicular tower of the Cistercian abbey reaching towards the white and blue sky.'

Mrs Crowther begins to muse on what life would have been like for the monks in mediaeval times. As she does, she provokes her husband into a description of their nightly devotions.

Other 'Crowther' novels followed, but for the purpose of this journey it is useful to turn from this series of novels to other works that Armstrong set in the former North Riding. He lived at Askrigg for several years before moving to Low Row in Swaledale, so he knew the Dales as well as he knew the industrial West Riding.

Adam Brunskill (1952) tells how a young man bearing this name returns to his family's former village in Swaledale. He is a skilled lead miner and wishes to make a new life for himself in his home county. A feud between his father and his mother's brothers forced his father to live and work in a mining settlement in Spain. The mine owner there also had mines in North Yorkshire and so, after his father's death, Adam returns to England.

The novel not only gives a clear picture of the working life and conditions in the old lead mines — the rivalry between some of the workers and the dangers they encounter from natural hazards like water — but it also reveals the superstitions some of the men believe in about the 'owd man', a kind of malignant force that is determined to thwart the miners' efforts to make a living for themselves and their families.

Adam faces crisis after crisis at work and in his personal life, but he never loses his innate courage and cheerfulness. He is constantly encouraged throughout his struggles by Hannah Batty, the eighty-seven year old shopkeeper who also knew his parents. She wills him on to succeed in everything he undertakes, and gives him as much practical help as she can.

Whatever plot he constructed, Thomas Armstrong always thoroughly investigated the background of the industries, localities and types of people in his quest for authenticity. In his West Riding-based novels, that background was already ingrained in him through his early life in the local textile industry. Those who have studied the history of lead mining in the Dales and the archaeology of the mines still in existence can vouch for the authenticity of *Adam Brunskill,* a book many have declared to be his finest novel.

Although it is often difficult to convey a convincing atmosphere in novels set hundreds of years ago, *The Face of the Madonna* (1964) does succeed in depicting the North Yorkshire of the fourteenth century. This was a time when the abbeys and priories were at their most powerful, but when the Lollards — followers of John Wycliffe — were trying to undermine their power. The main characters are Ughtred, a young monk from Rievaulx Abbey, and Lazette, a beautiful young nun of Wootton Priory. Other memorable figures include the Lord Abbot and his kinswoman, the worldly Lady Prioress of Wootton; and, more important with regard to the plot, the travelling Friar Jerome with his herbal nostrums.

Like his other books, *The Face of the Madonna* contains accurately researched historical detail with a strong storyline and authentic characters, portraying what Armstrong termed the 'two Yorkshires in one county'.

An author who has done much to bring the beauty and tranquility of the Dales and its many characters to a wider audience only came to Yorkshire in early adulthood. Though a Scot, over the years James Herriot has influenced millions of people all over the world to discover and appreciate for themselves the area of the Dales around Askrigg, Richmond, Thirsk and Harrogate.

Born in 1916, after qualifying as a veterinary surgeon from Glasgow Veterinary College he came to Yorkshire in 1940 to join a practice in Thirsk. His many experiences, tinged with the affection and humour he gradually felt for the Dales people — not to mention their animals — became the basis of the writing career he took up thirty years later. His word pictures of the scenery were evocative descriptions of the various dales he grew to love, but the genuine glimpses into farming life there gave another dimension to his stories for those readers who lived in towns and cities. After the film and television adaptations of his work were made, this dimension provided a visual glimpse into what for most people was a different way of life amid the unspoilt beauty of the Dales.

Like many other authors, James Herriot uses composite portraits for much of the background to his novels. For example, he has stated that Darrowby, the imaginary name he gives to the place where he first starts practising, is a mixture of Askrigg, Thirsk, Richmond and his imagination. In his first book *If Only They Could Talk* (1970), he describes his first journey to Darrowby. He has never visited Yorkshire before, but confesses he was prepared for 'solid worth, dullness'. Anyone who remembers the pre-1939 Dales buses will recollect the friendly informality of the drivers, the vehicles owned by local firms, and their sometimes bumpy drives along rough roads. But such buses had a charm all of their own, especially when the driver got out to deliver a parcel to a wayside cottage, or newspaper to a village shop.

As he makes his first journey through the Dales, he begins to revise his preconceived ideas about his new home. Suddenly the bus stops in a cobbled market square. Over one shop he reads Darrowby Co-operative Society — 'we had arrived'. In the TV versions of his books, Skeldale House was in reality a large stone-built house in Askrigg. (It is now an Abbeyfield Home.) From that house-cum-surgery came a whole series of incidents arising from the daily life and experiences of a Dales vet and his colleagues, captured in such books as *It Shouldn't Happen to a Vet* (1972), *Vets Might Fly* (1976) and *The Lord God Made Them All* (1981).

Throughout all his novels, James Herriot has done much to convey to people who have never visited the region something of its impressive scenery and great beauty, and in this way has carried on the tradition of those writers from the Dales's literary past who grew to love what is widely regarded as the most picturesque part of Yorkshire.

West Yorkshire

Now to turn from the relatively unspoilt landscape of the Dales and Craven to what is now West Yorkshire but which until recently comprised, along with South Yorkshire, the Yorkshire industrial heartland of the West Riding. From the fourteenth century onwards, when Edward III enticed Dutch woollen and clothing workers to come to this country and bring their skills with them, the region has prospered. As early as 1642, Lord Clarendon in his *History of the Rebellion* described Halifax, Leeds and Bradford as ''three very populous and rich towns, depending wholly on clothes'.

Despite its abiding image as a mass of dark, forbidding mills and rows of cobbled streets, West Yorkshire's history is not solely based on industry, but has one of the strongest literary traditions in the whole country.

The office of 'Poet Laureate' as it is known today was first officially granted to Ben Jonson in 1616 when he was given a yearly sum of money by James I. In return, the recipient was meant to write poems for royal occasions, such as marriages and births. Though this is now no longer strictly enforced, the position is still a great honour.

In another hundred years or so, plaques will probably be erected in the Pennine towns of Mytholmroyd, Hebden Bridge and Heptonstall to notify visitors that Ted Hughes, the Poet Laureate since 1984, was born and raised in the area.

Mytholmroyd is a pleasant Calder Valley village, but with rugged moorlands encroaching almost into its very heart. Visitors walk over the small stone bridge, passing the parish church on one side of the road, before they arrive at a narrow street of sturdy stone houses and small shops. Further on, in the prettiest part, are flats and larger houses, and beyond them the beauties of Crag Vale.

There seems little indication at present that in August 1930, Edward James Hughes was born at 1 Aspinall Street, one of the terrace houses not far from the Rochdale Canal. He spent the first seven years of his life here in the Calder Valley. It is mainly a manufacturing district, but beyond the narrower industrialised valley are wooded slopes and crags and further away still are the moors. Long before the area became the tourist centre it is today, these provided favourite climbs and walks for the young boy and his brother, especially on their hunting and fishing trips.

Ted Hughes was only seven when his family moved to Mexborough — then part of the West Riding but now in South Yorkshire — where his father kept a newsagent's shop. The Jesuits believe that the experiences of a child's first seven years indelibly influence his later life. If this is so, then Ted Hughes's literary outlook would have been fixed before he became a pupil at Mexborough Grammar School. It was here he first began to write poetry when he was about fifteen years old. A few years later he won a scholarship to Pembroke College, Cambridge. National Service was still compulsory for young men, however, so he joined the Royal Air force before going to Cambridge.

From then on his interest in poetry quickened. He worked in several jobs, including teaching, but still continued to write. T S Eliot, then a director at Faber and Faber, was one of the first to recognise Hughes's poetic gifts. His first volume of verse, *A Hawk in the Rain,* was published by Faber and Faber in 1957, and immediately attracted much critical acclaim; it was the Poetry Book Society's choice of that year, and won the First Publication Award of the Poetry Society of New York when it was published in the USA.

In 1956 the young poet married American-born Sylvia Plath, whom he had met at university. For several years they lived in America, where for a while he taught creative writing at the University of Massachusetts. They returned to this country in 1959, and moved to Devon in 1961. During this time Ted Hughes's parents were living again in the Hebden Bridge area in a house called The Beacon. In her correspondence Sylvia mentions often staying in this part of West Yorkshire where she preferred the landscape and air to that of the sea.

Sylvia herself also had a short but distinguished career as a writer,

The Pennine village of Mytholmroyd, near Hebden Bridge.

The nearest house, 1 Aspinall Street, is the birthplace of Ted Hughes.

Phyllis Bentley.

with a collection of poems *The Colossus* (1960) and her only novel *The Bell Jar* (1963). The latter appeared only a month before she committed suicide in February 1963, and she is now buried in Heptonstall churchyard.

Ted Hughes's second volume, *Lupercal* (1960), proved to be an even greater success than his first and was awarded the Hawthornden Prize in 1961. (This award, founded in 1919, is granted to British authors of imaginative literature under forty-one years old.) At the time of the book's publication, Leonard Clark, literary critic of the *Yorkshire Post,* prophesied that if Ted Hughes continued to write poetry and develop 'at his present rate, he has a glowing future'.

How well that prophecy came true can be seen by his subsequent success, being awarded the Queen's Medal for Poetry in 1974 and the OBE in 1977, and culminating in succeeding John Betjeman as Poet Laureate in 1984.

His subsequent volumes of verse include *Wodwo* (1967); *Crow* (1970) a sequence of inter-related poems illustrated by the American artist Leonard Baskin; and *Moortown,* published in 1979. He has also written many books for children. *How the Whale Became* (1961) is a collection of stories; his poetry includes *Meet My Folks!* (1961); and he also edited *Poetry in the Making: An Anthology of Poems and Programmes.*

Many of his poems have been inspired by his early years in the Calder Valley. *Lupercal* includes *Pennines in April,* which imagines what would happen if the county of Yorkshire were a sea, and ends that it:

'Must burst upwards and topple into Lancashire.'

Wodwo, a collection of poetry and prose dedicated to his parents, contains a poem about Heptonstall. He calls it a 'Black village of gravestones', and ends on a rather dreary but unfortunately very true note that 'only the rain never tires'.

In *Remains of Elmet* (1979), with photographs by Fay Godwin, he portrays the decline of the basic industries of the Calder Valley, and its unchanging landscape. Elmet was the name of an ancient British kingdom in part of what is now West Yorkshire — the name lives on in such places as Sherburn-in-Elmet and Barwick-in-Elmet near

Leeds — and which he describes as 'the last British kingdom to fall to the Angles'. The book also contains a poem about Haworth, although many Brontë devotees will not relish the idea of the Brontë girls being described as 'Three weird sisters'.

In the late 1960's, Ted Hughes lived in a converted millowner's house near Heptonstall, and in 1970 this became the northern premises of the Arvon Foundation, into which he put much endeavour. Although he and his second wife Carol no longer reside at Lumb Bank, they continue to take a keen and practical interest in the running of the enterprise. Young writers can stay for a week here, meeting eminent authors and poets who offer them advice and encourage their writing efforts.

One of the earliest authors to have links with the region was, like Ted Hughes, educated at Pembroke College, Oxford. Sir Thomas Browne also wrote his most famous work, *Religio Medici,* while living in the Calder Valley town of Halifax. He was born on the 19th October 1605 in London, and died on that same date in 1682 in Norwich, where he was a well-respected physician. After leaving Oxford he spent time abroad where he studied medicine. He must have been a most industrious scholar, for his knowledge of six languages enabled him to learn a great deal about the countries he visited. His desire for learning embraced a wide range of subjects, and years later he advised his son Edward to show an equal enthusiasm for knowledge.

On his return to England he lived at Upper Shibden Hall near Halifax, and some time around 1635 for his own enjoyment started to write his first, and greatest, work *Religio Medici.* This gives his views on a variety of topics such as God and faith, prejudice of all kinds, and friendship. He observed:

'It was penned in such a place and with such disadvantages that (I protest) from the first setting of pen to paper I had not the assistance of any good book.'

This statement is corroborated by the scholar Richard Bentley (1662-1742), born in Oulton near Leeds, who wrote:

'...the author fixed himself in this populous and rich trading place wherein to show his skill and gain respect in the world; and that during his residence amongst us, and in his vacant hours, he wrote his admired piece "Religio Medici". Because it was written for his own private exercise and enjoyment, Thomas Browne expressed his deepest feelings and when completed had a few handwritten copies made...'

As with many early printed books a pirated edition was published in 1642, but it was reprinted the following year with additions by Browne himself. By the time the book became a success, the author was living in Norwich, having left Halifax in 1637. He was subsequently knighted by Charles II, and became friends with many famous people of the day. He was buried in St Peter Mancroft Church in Norwich, and there is a statue nearby to this learned man whose most important work was written in Halifax.

A writer already met in the chapter on York is Daniel Defoe who — while fleeing from the persecution he endured because of some of his writings — is reputed to have written part of *Robinson Crusoe* while staying at the Rose and Crown in Back Lane, Halifax. In his *1822 Directory,* the Leeds author and publisher Edward Baines stated:

'The celebrated Daniel De Foe, though not a native of Halifax, being obliged to abscond from his own neighbourhood on account of his political writings, came to this town, and enjoyed himself in writing — and in particular he is said to have composed here his famous romance of "Robinson Crusoe".'

Defoe was very interested in Halifax and he writes at great length about it in his *Tour.* He describes his journey into the town:

'...the nearer we came to Halifax, we found the houses thicker, and the villages greater in every [valley] bottom; and not only so, but the sides of the hills, which were very steep every way, were spread with houses, and that very thick.'

He is fascinated by the industrial life of the town and even as early as the eighteenth century it is clear that the region is prospering:

'The business is the clothing trade, for the convenience of which the houses are thus scattered and spread upon the sides of the hills'.

Defoe thinks the reason for this is because two of the raw materials for making cloth, coal and running water, are found 'upon the tops of the highest hills'. He comments:

'...such has been the bounty of nature to this otherwise frightful country...'

What Defoe called 'frightful country' has nevertheless been the birthplace of two of the most prolific and successful authors of modern times, J S Fletcher and Phyllis Bentley.

Although Joseph Smith Fletcher (1863-1935) was born in Halifax, his father, who was a nonconformist minister, died when Joseph was only eight months old and so the baby was brought up by relations at Darrington, near Pontefract. Determined from an early age to be a writer, he went to London at eighteen years old to work as a newspaper sub-editor for a guinea a week. Even in the latter part of the last century such a sum was unlikely to make him a fortune, so he tried his hand at freelance writing. Fletcher was not afraid of hard work, indeed one criticism of him today is that he wrote too much, too quickly.

The year 1893 saw the publication of a small volume of poems entitled *Poems Chiefly Against Pessimism.* A critic of the time wrote:

'There are few persons who read the book who will not admit that it contains not only promise of the future, but is of much present merit.'

The first poem sets the tone for the rest of the book:

'This my creed remains whatever
I may be, whatever doing.
Life's a time for glad endeavour,
Constant effort, all pursuing
Purposeful attempts to be
With nature in true harmony.
This my creed is, then, for ever.
Spite of all the ills we're heir to,
Joy must crown the strong endeavour
And the tasks this lead us thereto...'

In the years after leaving his newspaper employment his output was prolific. He seemed to be able to turn his pen to any subject, though his own keen interest in history and antiquarian matters helped to provide him with many facts and ideas. He wrote historical novels, biographies (including one on Cardinal Newman), dozens of short stories, books about Yorkshire and, towards the end of his career, detective novels.

From 1890 to 1900 he contributed a series under the pen-name 'Son of the Soil' to the *Leeds Mercury*. In 1892 appeared the first volume of his highly regarded historical novel *When Charles the First was King,* which was what was known as a 'three-decker' and was published in a single volume in 1894. It has always been regarded as one of the finest — if not the finest — of his works. Amongst his Yorkshire non-fiction was *A Picturesque History of Yorkshire* (three volumes from 1889 to 1891). *All About Yorkshire* (1900) and *The Cistercians in Yorkshire* (1919). Some scholars regard his historical non-fiction work as not profound enough; other readers admire the books.

Later in his career he wrote many detective novels, and one of these, *The Middle Temple Murder,* was highly admired by the American President Woodrow Wilson. This success led Fletcher into a new career as a popular detective novelist. An indication of the breadth of his writing is that a collection of his poems from 1881 onwards was published in 1931. Yet this industrious Yorkshire author's fame surely rests on the fine historical novels set in his home county.

As we have seen, Halifax's prosperity rested on the textile industry, from the cottage industries as depicted by Defoe to the large textile mills of the nineteenth and twentieth centuries which Phyllis Bentley (1894-1977) used as the basis for her most memorable work. Born in a house on Stanley Road, Halifax, her father was a textile manufacturer, so in a way the little girl had all her background material to hand well before she was mature enough to use it — though use it she later did in her textile-based novels. Even when small she enjoyed putting ideas into words; at six years old she gave her father a poem, but sold a story for three pence to her older brother a few years later. Educated at Halifax High School and Cheltenham Ladies College, she soon became a published author with *Environment* (1922), followed a year later by *Cat-in-the-Manger*.

Such limited successes did not satisfy her ambitions, and she decided to write a long novel, authentically researched, about the textile industry from the days of the Luddites to modern times. (The Luddites were a body of men who, between 1812 and 1818, toured the north of England and smashed up the newly-introduced machinery they felt would take away their livelihood. They were named after Ned Ludd, who led the first attack in the Midlands.) Woven into the fabric of the novel would be the lives of different families. This was a subject she knew thoroughly, and she could be said to have known all sides since she knew both workers and employers. She was also familiar with the disruptive forces that can cause havoc in the industry; her family had experienced the troubled times of the late 1920's and early 1930's. Out of her family background, interests and research emerged *Inheritance* (1932).

Before she began the novel she decided that if it did not meet with success she would find another career. She had had some experience as both a teacher and librarian so this would not be difficult, but her wish was still to be a successful author. She had no need to fear, as *Inheritance* became one of the most popular novels of the time.

During an interview in the early 1950's she told the writer, 'The effect of time on character fascinates me'. She went on to maintain:

'What a person is at one point in his or her life and what he or she is twenty-years later — what has happened to cause the change — that's life to me.'

That fascination with cause and effect helped to strengthen *Inheritance,* as it did her later work. Other novels were added to her textile saga, including *The Rise of Henry Morcar* (1946), *A Man of His Time* (1966) and her final story dealing with the characters met earlier in previous novels, *Ring in the New* (1970). She also wrote many absorbing short stories, including her *Tales of the West Riding* and *More Tales of the West Riding.*

Anyone wishing to read a brief history of the textile trade cannot do better than read chapter twenty-nine of *The Rise of Henry Morcar.* Even when taken out of context it gives a short word-picture of how the trade evolved in the Pennines. Henry Morcar, a successful manufacturer who nevertheless has had a rough business struggle in his early years, meets young David Oldroyd, one of the descendants of old Mr Oldroyd who was murdered by the Luddites in the first chapters of *Inheritance*. The Oldroyd mills have suffered during the slump of the 1930's, and David's father Francis has retired to the south. But his son is determined to return to his native area and rebuild the firm. With his cousins the Mellors (who are descended from one of the Luddite characters) they start up in business in Old Syke Mills.

Strangely enough for a successful manufacturer, Henry Morcar seems ignorant of the historical background of his industry. He visits David's home, a converted weaver's cottage with a long loom chamber upstairs where one of the young man's ancestors lived in Luddite days. During the visit, David explains something of the textile industry in the area and how the physical landscape of the Pennines, with its plentiful streams and good rainfall, was ideal for cloth manufacturing. As part of the chronicles of a textile landscape this chapter is fascinating.

Phyllis Bentley wrote other novels which also dealt with local trade and industry. *A Modern Tragedy* (1933) depicts how an unscrupulous but expert manufacturer involves the young, ambitious Walter Haigh in his efforts to keep his business financially viable. The day of reckoning arrives of course, and with his partner Leonard Tasker, Walter has to take a share of the blame for the unlawful practices. The authoress emphasised that this novel's events were in no way the description of a true event, but pointed out that the disaster which befell the fictitious characters could easily happen in real life.

One of her earliest novels, *Carr* (1929), was written as if it was a biography of Philip Joseph Carr by his grand-daughter. Again the 'author's note' maintains that the town of Hudley and the village of Carr Foot are all entirely imaginary, but later she does confess that the characters of Philip Carr and his wife were based on her parents — though their circumstances were entirely different. One of her mother's ancestors, who founded Hanson's School in Bradford and was a pioneer of education, also became the model for Joth Bamforth in *Inheritance*.

She derived inspiration from many sources — old graveyards would provide her with surnames — and some of her plots came about unexpectedly. For example, in 1952 she was walking on the moors and came to a remote hill in a valley which eventually became the Wool Royd of *The House of the Morays* (1954), set in the eighteenth century.

In 1970 she was awarded the OBE for her services to literature. She had travelled widely abroad, most often to America on lecture tours, but her home remained the West Riding town where she still had firm roots and many interests, including the local thespians. For many years she lived at 8 Heath Villas in Halifax, but in 1970 moved to a seventeenth century farmhouse that had once been the home of a yeoman farmer and clothier. Could any building have been more appropriate for the woman who had made her own area and its textile industry come alive in novels now read all over the world?

It would be impossible to ignore the world famous Brontë family in any account of the Yorkshire's literary heritage. Their story covers so much of the region, as seen in the survey of the east coast, but most notably the West Riding. Here many of the places of interest are close enough to be visited in one day, but each is also worthy of a longer and more detailed exploration.

The story began when the Reverend Patrick Brontë, born in Ireland in 1777, proposed marriage to Penzance-born Miss Maria Branwell in the grounds of Kirkstall Abbey, just outside Leeds. They were subsequently married at Guiseley Parish Church on the 29th December 1812. The announcement of the marriage appeared in the *Gentleman's Magazine* in early 1913.

'Lately at Guiseley, near Bradford, by the Rev W Morgan, minister of Bierley, the Rev Patrick Brontë BA, minister of Hartshead-cum-Clifton to Maria, third daughter of the late T Branwell, Esq of Penzance. And at the same time by the Rev P Brontë, Rev W Morgan to the only daughter of the Rev John Fennell, headmaster of the Wesleyan Academy, near Bradford.'

The latter is now better known as Woodhouse Grove School, Rawdon. John Fennel was Maria Branwell's uncle, and it was while visiting her relations that she was introduced to Patrick Brontë by the Rev W Morgan.

Before his marriage, Mr Brontë had been the curate at Dewsbury parish church, which stands near the centre of this industrial town, from 1809 to 1811. In 1811 he moved to Hartshead, and to where he brought his bride. They lived at Clough House, Hightown, near the church, and it was here that their first two children Maria and Elizabeth were born. In 1815, Mr Brontë exchanged livings with the Rev Thomas Atkinson of Thornton. This was a chapel-of-ease known as the Old Bell Chapel and attached to Bradford parish church. The five years the Brontë family spent in Thornton were very happy ones.

Several years ago an elderly Thornton resident observed to the writer:

'It's time people remembered Thornton. After all, all four of the famous Brontës were born here.'

More recently, Thornton's associations with the family have been emphasised, much of it due to the present Vicar of Thornton, the Rev Peter Fordham.

Previously the only indication of their time here was the unveiling of a memorial tablet in 1916 in St James's Church on Thornton Road. It celebrated:

> '1816. In Memoriam. 1916.
> To the inspiring Memory and Genius of
> Charlotte Brontë
> Author of Jane Eyre. Shirley. Villette.
> And in Commemoration of the Centenary
> of her Birth at Thornton on April 21 1816.
> During the five years that her father
> the Reverend Patrick Brontë AB exercised his
> Ministry here his four gifted children were born
> and were Baptized in the old Thornton Chapel
> nigh to this Church.
> Charlotte ("Currer Bell") 1816. Patrick Branwell 1817.
> Emily Jane ("Ellis Bell") 1818. Anne ("Acton Bell") 1820.'

The tablet goes on to state that the memorial was 'Erected by Thornton People in Time of European War 1916'.

Also inside the church is the font where the four babies were baptised. Built after the Brontës left Thornton to replace the Old Bell Chapel, St James's Church was consecrated on the 21st August 1872 and had its own font. When Mr Fordham came to Thornton he had a mobile frame made into which was fixed the 'Brontë font', since many parents like their children to be baptized in the same font as the Brontë children. At one time kept in the porch, it is now near the chancel and is moved to the front of the chancel for baptisms.

Mr Brontë conducted services in the little Old Bell Chapel across the now busy road, and he improved the building a great deal. Quite a section of the chapel remained even at the end of the last century, but now only the bell turret and a low foundation wall mark the place of worship known to the Brontës. The white dove and orb that once graced the top of Mr Brontës three-decker pulpit is now on a window sill near St James's pulpit.

Thornton was only a tiny village when Mr and Mrs Brontë and their six children lived in the parsonage at 74 Market Street. Here a small iron tablet near the front door informs passers-by that the house is where four of the Brontë children were born in its front parlour. In its time the former parsonage has been a domestic dwelling, a butcher's shop and a gift and sweet shop. The section that included the shop window was built after the Brontës lived there.

The nearby countryside also has other associations with the family. Miss Elizabeth Firth of Kipping Hall — later the wife of the Vicar of Huddersfield — often used to take them on picnics to such places as Ogden, between Bradford and Halifax. Today this pleasant stretch of land is a country park.

In 1820, several carts packed with household belongings left Thornton Parsonage. They went by way of Denholme and Oxenhope to Haworth, where the Rev Patrick Brontë had been appointed perpetual curate. Their arrival in Haworth brought tremendous change into the lives of the children. Their mother died in 1821 and their aunt Miss Elizabeth Branwell came from Cornwall to take charge of the domestic side of the parsonage. She found the moorland village bleak to say the least.

An old view of Market Street, Thornton.

The arch, low boundary wall and bell turret are all that remains of
Thornton's Old Bell Chapel where the Rev Patrick Brontë was incumbent
from 1815 to 1820.

An old view of Haworth from the south-east. From Whiteley Turner's
A Spring Time Saunter.

An old view of Top Withens, now derelict, reputed to be the site of Emily
Brontë's *Wuthering Heights.* From *A Spring Time Saunter.*

The two eldest children Maria and Elizabeth both died in 1825 of typhus, which they had contracted while pupils of Cowan Bridge School in Casterton, Lancashire. The Rev Carus Wilson, founder of this school for the daughters of poor clergy, had very strict ideas about training children. He believed in obedience, hard work and endurance, and comfort of any kind was thought to be a hindrance to spiritual well-being. Charlotte was a pupil at Cowan Bridge, and saw the suffering her sister endured. When she came to write *Jane Eyre* she portrayed the school as Lowood School, and Mr Wilson as Mr Brocklehurst.

The later education of Charlotte, Emily and Anne was under Miss Margaret Wooler at Roe Head School, near Mirfield, and later the school moved to Healds House, Low Moor, Dewsbury. Here Charlotte met her two closest friends, Mary Taylor and Ellen Nussey. Charlotte later returned to Miss Wooler's school as a teacher from 1835 to the end of 1837.

While children at the parsonage, the Brontës wrote in minute script about the adventures of two imaginary countries, Angria and Gondal. Charlotte and Branwell were concerned with the former, while Emily and Anne concentrated on Gondal, supposedly an island in the South Pacific. Phyllis Bentley maintained that the themes which later appeared in Emily's *Wuthering Heights* (1847) are foreshadowed in her poems about Gondal.

Other influences played their part in that novel, however. Emily had been a teacher for a few months in 1837 at Miss Elizabeth Patchett's school, Law Hill near Southowram, Halifax. She was always homesick when away from Haworth, even when only a few miles away at Halifax. Some of the poetry she wrote at Law Hill expressed a yearning for the moors:

> '…lovelier than the cornfields all waving
> In emerald and scarlet and gold
> Are the slopes where the north wind is raving
> And the glens where I wandered of old.'

Law Hill had been built about 1771 by Jack Sharp, who had led a reckless life not unlike that of Heathcliff.

When she came to write her novel, Emily based the architecture of Wuthering Heights on High Sunderland Hall in the Shibden Valley, half a mile from Halifax. Before most of the hall was demolished some years ago, visitors could still see the little statues Emily mentions in her first description of Heathcliff's home.

Wuthering Heights begins rather bleakly with the date '1801'. Lockwood, the narrator of the novel, has become the tenant of Thrushcross Grange. (This was based on Ponden Hall, about two miles from Haworth, which was built in 1634 by the Heaton family, and which the Brontës no doubt visited as children.) He decides to walk to the nearby residence to greet his new landlord, Heathcliff:

'Wuthering Heights is the name of Mr Heathcliff's dwelling, and "Wuthering" being a significant provincial adjective descriptive of the atmosphere's building to which its situation is exposed in windy weather...

The architect had foresight to build it strong; all narrow windows are deeply set in the wall and corners defended with large jutting stones...

Before passing the threshold I paused to admire a quantity of grotesque carvings over the front, and especially above the principal door above which amongst a wilderness of crumbling griffins and shameless little boys, I detected the date "1500" and the name "Heaton Earnshaw".'

Lockwood's second visit took place in wintry weather. He was tempted to stay at home, but:

'...I took my hat and, after a four mile walk arrived at Heights' garden gate just in time to escape the first feather flake of a snow storm...On the bleak hill-top the earth was hard with a black frost and the air made me shiver through every limb.'

Though its architectural model may have been High Sunderland Hall, the location of Wuthering Heights is thought to be Top Withens, south-west of Haworth. But if this is its setting, the ruined building that now stands there and attracts so many visitors was certainly not the model for Heathcliff's home. In fact Top Withens was once little more than a simple farmhouse dwelling, similar to many others in the area. In 1964 the Brontë Society had a tablet fixed to the side of Top Withens which read:

'This farmhouse has been associated with "Wuthering Heights", the Earnshaw home of Emily Brontë's novel. The buildings even when complete bore no resemblance to the house she described; but the situation may have been in her mind when she wrote of the moorland setting of the "Heights".'

Returning to the Brontës themselves, the sisters experienced disappointment before they became successful authors. The book of poems they paid to have published in 1846 sold only a few copies. Charlotte's first novel *The Professor* was then submitted to a publisher, along with those of her sisters, Emily's *Wuthering Heights* and Anne's *Agnes Grey*. Their identities were protected by pseudonyms, Charlotte being Currer Bell, Emily, Ellis Bell and Anne was Acton Bell. The novels of the two latter were accepted for publication, *The Professor* was not. (It was later published two years after Charlotte's death in 1857.) Instead Charlotte began to write *Jane Eyre,* and when completed she submitted it to Smith Elder — a far more distinguished publisher than the one who still retained her sisters' novels. *Jane Eyre* appeared in October 1847, and Emily and Anne's novels were published later in the same year. All three girls experienced the happiness of successful authorship, though because of their pseudonyms few knew of their achievements.

Even so, severe personal troubles faced them. Branwell, whose dissolute lifestyle had been a constant source of anxiety to his father and sisters, died on the 24th September 1848; soon after Emily died on the 19th December 1848 and Anne in Scarborough the following May.

Charlotte completed her novel *Shirley* soon after Anne's death (she had begun it before the bereavement), and it was published in August 1849. Its Spen Valley setting was so vividly described that a Haworth man living in Liverpool knew at once it was someone from his native town that had written the book. He could think of no other likely person than the parson's daughter, Charlotte. Proud of his theory, he wrote to a Liverpool paper outlining it, and the secret leaked out:

Currer Bell, the author of two novels, was in fact Charlotte Brontë. Even the novelist must have gained some amusement, for she observed:

'...the Haworthians are making great fools of themselves about "Shirley". They enjoyed picking out real settings and the people they thought had been portrayed in the novel.'

One person who also derived much amusement at the antics of the curates described in the novel was Mr Brontë's curate and Charlotte's future husband, the Rev Arthur Bell Nicholls. He laughed so much that his landlady began to fear he was going mad.

By this time only Charlotte and her father were living at the parsonage, attended by their devoted servant Martha Brown. Charlotte's life became more fulfilled. She corresponded with other famous authors, and paid visits to the radical journalist Harriet Martineau in the Lake District, and the Kay-Shuttleworths at Gawthorpe Hall, Lancashire, to name but a few of her new friends.

Another new friend was the novelist Mrs Elizabeth Gaskell. They first met in 1850, and in her *Life of Charlotte Brontë* — begun in 1855 and published two years later — Mrs Gaskell tells of her first visit to Haworth. Writing on the 1st June 1853, Charlotte invited her for a visit, which did not materialise until the end of September. Mrs Gaskell described her first impression of the parsonage as being:

'...an oblong stone house facing over the hill on which the village stands and with the front door right opposite to the western door of the church — distance about a hundred yards.'

The parsonage was at that time without the tall wing which was added by Mr Brontë's successor, the Rev John Wade, who hated sightseers looking into his windows. Mrs Gaskell observed:

'...there is a pleasant old fashioned custom of window seats all through the house and one can see that the parsonage was built when wood was plentiful, as the massive stair banisters and the wainscots and the heavy windows testify...'

The atmosphere of the house also delighted her. She wrote:

'I don't know that I ever saw a spot more exquisitely clean; the most dainty place for that I ever saw. To be sure the life is like clockwork.

Charlotte Brontë, c.1854.

Oakwell Hall, Birstall, the prototype for Fieldhead in Charlotte Brontë's
novel *Shirley*.

Mr Brontë's study.

The kitchen at the parsonage.

No one comes to the house; nothing disturbs the deep repose; hardly a voice is heard; you catch the ticking of the clock in the kitchen, the buzzing of a fly in the parlour...'

There was not much this accomplished novelist and kind-hearted woman missed. She described the furnishings:

'The parlour has been evidently refurnished within the last few years, since Miss Brontë's success has enabled her to have a little more money to spend. Everything fits into, and is in keeping with the idea of a country parsonage possessed by people of very moderate means. The prevailing colour of the room is crimson, to make a warm setting for the cold grey landscape without. There is her likeness to Richmond and an engraving of Lawrence's picture of Thackeray and the two recesses on each side of the high narrow old-fashioned mantel-piece filled with books — books given to her, books she has bought and which tell of her individual pursuits and tastes; not standard books.'

Although the Rev A B Nicholls had been wanting to marry Charlotte for some time, the wedding did not take place until the 29th June 1854 due to her indecision and her father's opposition. Between his unsuccessful courtship and her acceptance of him he had moved to another curacy, but returned later. Sadly Charlotte died only nine months after her marriage in 1855, and was pregnant at the time.

Mrs Gaskell visited the parsonage again after Charlotte's death to collect information for her forthcoming biography. Although she treated Mr Brontë rather unjustly in her account of the Brontë's family life, he often excused her to friends and the few visitors he consented to see by observing that 'she was a novelist and therefore to be excused for taking rather dramatic views of events'. (However Mr Nicholls was not quite so forgiving!) Mr Brontë lived on until the 7th June 1861 when at the age of eighty-four he died, having outlived all his children.

Shortly after Charlotte's death, the poet and critic Matthew Arnold wrote the poem *Haworth Churchyard*. It presents a very dismal picture, and part of it reads:

'...lonely and bleak at its side,
The parsonage house and the graves.'

At that time Haworth's old church was still in existence. It was Mr Brontë's successor, Rev John Wade, who campaigned for it to be demolished for health reasons, and it was rebuilt in 1881. Only the tower now remains of the St Michael and All Angels Church known to the Brontë household, though the bells re-hung in the tower in 1988 date back to Mr Brontë's time. The tenor bell bears the inscription:

'These bells were raised by subscription AD 1845 Rev Patrick Brontë AB Incumbent and Mr Geo. Feather and Mr Jas. Lambert churchwardens.'

Anyone visiting Haworth today and hearing the bells know that they are listening to a sound the Brontës would have often heard over a century and a half ago. The church itself contains many fine associations with the Brontës, including the memorial chapel and the vault where all of the family — excluding Anne — were laid to rest.

Some idea of what Haworth and its surroundings were like in the last century can be gleaned from reading *Haworth Past and Present* (1897) by the Yorkshire historian and antiquarian J Horsfall Turner. In 1913 Whiteley Turner, another topographical author, gave a fascinating account of his walks and explorations around Bradford and Haworth in *A Springtime Saunter*. Both these books are ideal background reading for anyone wishing to gain an impression of Haworth before it became a modern tourist centre.

Interest in the Brontës had increased during the latter half of the nineteenth century. The Brontë Society was founded in 1893, and there was soon a small museum above the Penny Bank in Main Street. This was opened in 1895, and according to a contemporary report, as well as Haworth Brass Band, there were 'flags flying and special trains from Bradford and the Heavy Woollen district'. Tom Bradley in his book *Jacksons's Cycle Rides* advised any people intent on doing the 'run' to Haworth to call in at the little museum that had just been opened, and stated:

'The place has been frequented by a vast number of visitors since its opening and should on no account be missed.'

Successive incumbents of Haworth continued to live in the parsonage until a new rectory was built further on towards the moors, and the parsonage put up for sale in the late 1920's. It was bought by the Haworth-born industrialist Sir James Roberts, and presented to the Brontë Society in 1928. It was re-opened as the Brontë Parsonage Museum by Lady Roberts on the 4th August of that year — only fitting considering that she had suggested to her husband he should make the purchase in the first place.

To commemorate the sixtieth anniversary of its opening, a stone has been fixed to the boundary wall of the parsonage garden where the churchyard gate used to be. Nearby is a rough boulder, marking the opening of the museum. The garden itself has been redesigned with plants and flowers of the type that would have been growing in Haworth and the surrounding village gardens over a hundred years ago. A new sign near the entrance gate also marks the anniversary, but the familiar wrought-iron sign attached to the gable end of the building and overhanging the narrow lane leading to the moors still remains. It depicts Charlotte seated at a table, pen in hand; designed by Mr Harold Mitchell, the long-serving first custodian of the Parsonage Museum, it was made by a local blacksmith.

Since the sign was erected, hundreds of thousands of people from all over Britain and the rest of the world — including Japan, where there is a very keen interest in the Brontës — have visited Haworth. They visit the nearby moors, where walks to Top Withens and the Brontë Waterfall provide an invigorating tramp for many people. At the latter place, visitors will remember that it was a favourite spot with all of the Brontë girls. Charlotte's final walk before her fatal illness was to see the waterfall once more. She wrote to a friend how she and her husband visited the beauty spot in the depths of winter:

'It was fine indeed; a perfect torrent racing over the rocks, white and beautiful! It began to rain while we were watching it, and we returned home under a streaming sky. However, I enjoyed the walk inexpressibly, and would not have missed the spectacle on any account.'

However often one visits the parsonage, there always seems to be something different to see. It may have been overlooked on previous occasions, or an improvement or addition may have recently been made. Everything displayed in the house is a genuine Brontë article or has close associations with the family. The room arrangements are as near as possible to those of Brontë times, especially after Charlotte became more prosperous. Today it takes time to explore the old house and also to do justice to the fine exhibitions and displays in the extension to the museum. In order to mark its sixtieth anniversary the former curator, Dr Juliet Barker, has written and produced a book, *Sixty Treasures: The Brontë Parsonage Museum,* which features sixty of the most interesting exhibits in the museum, one for each year of its history.

The best time to visit Haworth itself is in late autumn, early spring or even in winter, for then the little town seems to be enjoying its own life. There is also time and more space to explore in search of the many links with the famous family.

Halliwell Sutcliffe, the novelist born at Thackley near Bradford already met in chapter three, also used the moors around Haworth as settings for some of his novels, notably *Ricroft of Withens* which features the Old Silent Inn at nearby Stanbury. He once considered making Ponden Hall his home:

'You shall never see such a house elsewhere; nor is it easy to describe the individual charm it has.'

His novel *By Moor and Fell* gives a charming picture of a family living there. His 'Wyngates' novels are set in the moorlands around here: Ponden Hall became his Wyngates, and nearby Ponden Reservoir is Sorrowful Water. Other novels set in the Wycoller, Colne and Haworth areas include *Mistress Barbara Cuncliffe, Through Sorrow's Gate* and *Lonesome Heights.*

Members of the Brontë family often walked from Haworth into nearby Keighley, and the Rev P Brontë visited it on occasion to borrow from the library of the local Mechanics' Institute. It was also in Keighley that G K Chesterton (1874-1936) discovered the prototype for his 'Father Brown' detective stories. Born in London, he made his name as a journalist and novelist, but his discovery of a new fictional character was quite accidental and resulted from a lecture given by Chesterton in Keighley. He stayed with the local Roman Catholic

The parsonage dining room, described by Mrs Gaskell.

The opening of the Brontë Parsonage Museum in 1928.

John Braine.

priest, Father John O'Connor. (Chesterton himself became a Roman
Catholic in 1922.) This priest's saintly demeanour seemed to survive
in spite of knowing so much more about what has been called the 'old
Adam' in human beings, especially amongst the criminal fraternity.
Chesterton moved his fictional Father Brown to East Anglia on his
first appearance in *The Innocence of Father Brown* (1911).

Chesterton did not attach much importance to the Father Brown
stories himself. It has been said that he used to write one or two
whenever he felt the need to make some extra money — often for the
many worthy causes he supported — but his stories of the quiet priest
who nevertheless has a keen and inquiring mind became very
popular, and are probably the best remembered of his works.

Keighley to Bingley is a journey of only a few miles and this West
Riding town was fictionalised as Warley by John Braine (1922-1986).
Born in Bradford, where his mother was a librarian, he was educated
at St Bede's Grammar School before taking various jobs, including
working in a bookshop, as a laboratory assistant and a spell in the
Royal Navy during the war. In 1949 he became assistant librarian at
Bingley Library, and was also involved with the production of
Bingley's Little Theatre.

In 1951 he moved to London to become a freelance writer, but
returned to Yorkshire later that year when his mother was killed in a
car accident. As a sufferer from TB he was a patient for eighteen
months in Grassington Sanatorium, where he began writing 'Joe for
King'. Even when it was completed and sent to various publishers he
faced disappointment, for it was rejected four times before being
accepted and published under its new title of *Room at the Top* in 1957.
Braine was now branch librarian of West Riding County Library, but
the novel's success meant he could take up writing as a career.

Room at the Top describes how a young man from a working class
background decides to reach a higher strata of society, 'the top', and
the means he employs to fulfil his ambitions provide an interesting
character study. Joe Lampton comes to work in Warley, a thinly
disguised Bingley, and falls in love with a married woman whom he
has met in a local theatre group. He does not wish to marry her even

if she seeks a divorce from her unfaithful husband, because Joe has decided that success for him can be furthered by marrying Susan Browne, the daughter of a local industrialist. He seduces Susan and marries her, and this prompts the suicide of his former lover.

That is a brief outline of the plot, but the strength and immediacy of Braine's writing quickly moved his first novel to the top of the best-seller lists in 1957. After publication it sold 5,000 copies in the first week, and over 25,000 by the end of three months. At the time of the novel's appearance, Britain was experiencing a relaxing in social attitudes, and with his story of the ruthless and ambitious Joe Lampton, John Braine was soon greeted as another 'angry young man' from the provinces.

After his great success John Braine moved south on account of his ill-health. Other novels followed, including *The Vodi* (1959), the sequel *Life at the Top* (1962) and *The Queen of a Distant Country* (1972) featuring the east coast, though none enjoyed quite the success of his first work. During November 1986, the West Yorkshire Archives Service in Bradford arranged a special memorial exhibition from its extensive collection of Braine's manuscripts and papers which provided the background to his writing life and work.

John Braine also wrote a fine biography of J B Priestley named simply after its subject, which was published in 1979 just a few years before Priestley's death. In his foreword, Braine stated that readers would soon realise that this most famous of Bradford's literary sons has much to offer them.

As befits its subject and by its very position in front of the National Museum of Photography, the statue of J B Priestley commands attention. Coat-tails flying, it conveys the impression that the stalwart Yorkshire writer is poised for a few minutes on a windy moorland before setting out once more to tramp across the beautiful Dales he loved so much. On the statue's base is an extract from his novel *Bright Day*.

John Boynton Priestley was born in Saltburn Place, Toller Lane, and attended Belle Vue Grammar School. He owed much of his early interest in literature to his schoolmaster father, Jonathan Priestley, who also installed into him the maxim: 'If you have more, you must give more.' Another great influence on the young John was a teacher, Richard Pendlebury. He later maintained that Mr Pendlebury possessed what he regarded as the highest teaching qualification — a love of good writing and the enthusiasm to communicate the subject to his pupils.

In one of his essays, Priestley tells how as a twelve year old boy he painstakingly produced a hand-written magazine containing first parts of several different stories, all written by himself. Having left school, he decided against trying for university and started work as a junior clerk for a wool merchant in Swan Arcade, Market Street. The arcade was swept away several years ago, much to the lasting indignation of its most famous ex-employee. In the colloquial phrase of his home county, he 'just couldn't get over it'. Later when he referred to his native city, he declared that his Bradford 'had died in 1914'.

His impressions of his early life in what was a hard-working northern city, yet one enlightened by many cultural attractions, can be read in some of his essays and *Bright Day* (1946). The novel begins with the affluent and well-known film-script writer Gregory Dawson, who is staying at a Cornish hotel. Two of his fellow guests seem familiar — surely he knew them years ago? They were Malcolm and Eleanor Nixley when young Gregory knew them in his home town of Bruddesford, but now they are titled. Nixley had arrived in Bruddesford to oversee the business where Gregory worked, and his youthful conclusion had been that the Nixleys had spoilt both the firm and his own happy relationship with the manager's family.

Many years later in Cornwall, he and the Nixleys make themselves known to each other. Through this re-meeting, Gregory Dawson vividly remembers pre-1914 Bruddesford, his early working life in a wool merchant's office and how he met the Allingtons, the manager's delightful family, who enchanted him with their knowledge of art, music, literature and the theatre. Their attitude to life in general had seemed to him far removed from the no-nonsense characteristics of many Yorkshire people. Even so, young Gregory had sometimes been amazed at the hidden side of the supposedly dour folk, such as works foreman Joe Ackworth's keen interest in rose-growing, and his hope of winning a major award at the Saltaire rose show. During the course of the novel, Gregory Dawson meets two members of the Allington family, but the former enchantment has now disappeared.

Like many novelists, Priestley maintained that his work was not based on any particular place or people, but was a composite picture from a variety of sources. However, his many readers rightly regard Bruddesford as Bradford's imaginary 'twin town'.

Side by side with Bradford's Yorkshire-born population dwelt people who had come from all over the world to live and work in the area; the city was famous for its district known as 'little Germany'. Priestley had an affection for many of the characteristics of Yorkshire people; their practical attitudes; their stubbornness on occasions; but also their innate kindness. Each an individual in his or her own right, in a county that admired individuality.

One area Priestley knew well was Manningham Lane, at that time one of the choicest residential districts. Named after the textile baron Samuel Cunliffe Lister, Lister Park (also called Manningham Park) is still a pleasant place, especially in spring when a wealth of flowers enrich the part that borders the now busy main road. It has associations with many Yorkshire writers besides the young Priestley. He later recollected the regular Sunday brass band concerts held there, and the broad pathway nearby known as the 'promenade' where the young people strolled.

During his early years in Bradford, Priestley first nurtured his love of drama, attending performances at the local theatres. One of these was the Theatre Royal on Manningham Lane. (At the time of writing there are plans to restore and refurbish what in his youth was a fine theatre.) It was known as the Royal Alexander when it opened on Boxing Day 1864 as there was already a Theatre Royal elsewhere in the town, but changed its name in 1868. Many famous actors and actresses of the day took part in performances there, probably the most famous being Sir Henry Irving, who in 1905 was taken ill whilst playing the lead role in *Becket* and died shortly afterwards in the

J B Priestley.

The Swan Arcade, Bradford, in 1900. This is where J B Priestley started work, the demolition of which greatly upset him.

Midland Hotel. The Playhouse was another favourite of J B Priestley, and his associations with this particular theatre continued many years after he left Bradford. The theatrical background he absorbed during this time must have been invaluable when he came to write his plays, which number around fifty.

Early in World War I, Priestley decided to join the armed forces and, as might be expected, he enlisted in the Duke of Wellington's regiment at Halifax. With the war over, he went to Trinity Hall, Cambridge, where he studied literature and modern history. For years he had cherished an ambition to become a writer, and even when working in the wool merchant's office he had dreamt of the day when he could rent a small cottage near Baildon Moor and earn enough to become a full-time writer — his financial target then was twenty-five shillings a week. He had already had pieces published by the local newspaper before the war, and his first book was a volume of poems published in 1914.

In 1922 he settled in London, continuing his journalism and having his first novel *Brief Diversions* published. It was well-received but did not make him a great deal of money. When he told his parents of his plans to become a full-time writer they were perturbed, anxious that he would not get a regular income. He soon proved them wrong, and many books followed his first efforts. Priestley always had plenty of ideas, but as he once maintained:

'Ideas are not much good without the persistence to carry them out.'

Priestley was one writer who had such persistence. His output was tremendous, covering plays, novels, essays, travel writing and criticism. He was equally at home with a variety of literary forms, and though never a 'regional' writer he always remembered his background and origins.

His early novel *Adam in Moonshine* (1926) has a Dales setting, and *The Good Companions* (1929) is the humorous story of a travelling theatre troupe, and features the town of Bruddesford. Richly peopled with diverse characters, including the unforgettable Jess Oakroyd, it was his first major success and soon became a bestseller. It is still popular today, and has been filmed for both the cinema and TV. In 1930 came *Angel Pavement,* a grimmer and more depressing account of life in London, followed by a host of other popular and critically-acclaimed novels such as *Let the People Sing* (1939), *The Magicians* (1954) and *Lost Empire* (1965).

With his plays he struck out in different directions: humorous, as depicted in *Laburnum Grove* (1933) and his West Riding-based comedy *When We Are Married* (1938), still a great favourite with both players and audiences in the north; and more serious, such as the psychological 'time thriller' *An Inspector Calls* (1947). Other plays with a strong time-related plot at which he excelled included *Dangerous Corner* (1932), *I Have Been Here Before* (1937) and *Time and the Conways* (1937).

Priestley was also a skilled practitioner at the art of writing essays. He often struck a 'grumbling' tone at the beginning of an essay, thereby grabbing the attention of the reader. An example of his simple and persuasive style is given in his *Essays of Five Decades* with an essay entitled 'The Unicorn', first published in a magazine in 1957. Priestley contrasts the difference between the image of the traditional British lion and that of the unicorn, and comes to the conclusion that if Britain wishes to retain its place as a world power then the time has come to adopt some of traits of the unicorn — imagination, creativity, individualism and inventiveness. Perhaps his comparisons are a little far-fetched, but his friendly and uncomplicated writing appealed to many people.

Probably Priestley's most famous non-fiction work is his account of his travels throughout England, *English Journey* (1934), which he described as:

'...a rambling, but truthful account of what one man saw, heard and felt.'

He declared that he had had the good fortune to have lived on some of the most beautiful and exciting country in England. The chapter 'A Sunday in the Dales' is still a delight to read.

In 1973 Bradford made J B Priestley a Freeman of the City, and in 1977 he was awarded the Order of Merit. But it was to his home county of Yorkshire that he returned after his death in 1984 when his

ashes were buried in a secret place in Hubberholme churchyard. A
month later a memorial tablet was unveiled to this modern 'man of
letters' in the little church of the tiny village he loved so much.

In 1911, at the same time that J B Priestley was spending his early
years in Bradford, Cardiff-born Howard Spring (1889-1968) joined
the *Yorkshire Observer* staff from the *South Wales News*. His first
impression of the city was the rattle over the stone setts of lorries piled
high with Bradford-made goods. The narrow streets and dour tall
buildings seemed strange to him in such a wealthy place. What Spring
did not then realise was that this grimy and functional background
had helped to create the city's wealth.

According to his own account, setting out to find accommodation
he bought an evening paper and took a one penny tram ride up to
Lister Park. He sat on a bench near the gateway and studied the lists
of rooms to let. One seemed suitable for him — and so it proved to
be, his new landlady having been a dresser to a variety stage
personality.

Soon afterwards he discovered the moors, taking a tram ride out of
the city and walking a few miles until he came to a rocky lane near an
inn where three roads met:

'I sat on a boulder patterned with lichens, and the shadows
thickened and far off the lights of the city came out upon the hills.'

The inn he mentioned was the Fleece, better known as Dick
Hudson's, after a nineteenth century landlord, famous for its meals
of ham and eggs provided for the ramblers coming out of Bradford
towards Ilkley Moor. Spring later featured this inn at High Eldwick
in his novel *Fame is the Spur*. He and his friends would sometimes visit
it for ham and egg breakfasts before going on to a local golf club.

Spring enjoyed his work as a journalist in Bradford — declaring the
paper a good one to work for — as well as the people he met and his
many experiences in the district. This, coupled with the opportunity
to read widely, caused him later to regard his Bradford years as his
'university'. In the second volume of his autobiography *In the
Meantime* (1942), he relates that he followed the same method of
reading as the Poet Laureate John Masefield had described in his

autobiography *In the Mill* (1941). A reviewer of Masefield's book had found the idea that reading one book leads to another as 'curious'. Spring did not agree:

'There is nothing curious in this. It is the usual procedure when the appetite of a voracious reader is once aroused, especially if he has no-one to guide him. It was my own fashion of proceeding from author to author in those Bradford days and was helped at any rate by the guidance of good conversation.'

Though he eventually moved away from Bradford, the experiences and impressions from his time there were later put to use in his novels, notably in his most famous work *Fame is the Spur* (1940). The young heroine Ann is banished from Manchester by her irate father to stay with her aunt, Lizzie Lighthowler, the widow of a prosperous wool merchant who lived along Manningham Lane. Strangely enough considering her background, Aunt Lizzie is a staunch socialist in the early days of the Labour movement. Through her activities, Ann meets two young Manchester men; Arnold she already knows, but his friend Hamer Shawcross is a new acquaintance. As the novel unfolds, we see that these two young men are entirely different in their outlook on life.

Baildon, High Eldwick and other places around Bradford are Howard Spring's literary landscape in the West Riding. Usually he employed the actual names of places and streets, for example Darley Street. Occasionally, however, he features the small market town of Smurthwaite and no doubt this is a composite picture of several such local towns.

It certainly proved an excellent setting for much of *These Lovers Fled Away* (1955). Young Chad Boothroyd, the narrator, and his widowed mother go to live with his uncle, Arthur Geldersome, the memorable town clerk of Smurthwaite. Their previous home has been in Cornwall, and when Chad's father is killed in an accident, Uncle Arthur brings them to Yorkshire. He and his sister, Chad's mother, had been brought up in Bradford where their father owned a chemist's shop on Manningham Lane. After a meal in the Midland Hotel they walk up to see their old home, and the next day they set off on a train journey to Smurthwaite. The scenery changes from an industrial landscape to green fields and fells terraced with white limestone:

'It [Smurthwaite] was a little place — it was one of those small country townships that somehow or other achieved the status of a borough...It is what I should call a solid, respectable, handsome little town.'

Chad goes on to describe the red sandstone castle that had been the home of the Newte family for hundreds of years. His life in Smurthwaite provides him with several friends, though their adult lives are set mainly in the south of England.

Smurthwaite turns up again in another of Spring's novels, *Time and the Hour* (1957). This opens in Manningham Lane, where young Chris Hudson lodges while his father does the round of local music halls as the impressionist 'The Great Hudson'.

After he left Bradford, Spring worked on the *Manchester Guardian* and later moved to London to become book reviewer for the *Evening Standard*. It was only after the great success of *My Son, My Son* in 1938 that he was able to turn to full time authorship, and he lived in Cornwall, first at Mylor Creek off the Truro Estuary and later in Falmouth.

As we have seen, not all the Brontës' associations are with Haworth. There are many links with what is called 'Shirley country' — the area of the Spen Valley, south-east of Bradford, around Birstall, Liversedge, Gomersal and Heckmondwike. This was used by Charlotte Brontë as the setting for her novel *Shirley* (1849), which Phyllis Bentley called 'the first Yorkshire regional novel'.

The plot of *Shirley* is connected with the introduction of machinery into the local textile mills around 1812, a development which provoked the Luddite riots. One of the most progressive and adamant mill owners in the Spen Valley was William Cartwright. He was not going to be intimidated by his work force and their associates from nearby towns, and was determined to install the cropping machines he had ordered. The riot featured in the chapter 'A Summer's Evening' actually took place at Rawford's Mill in Hunsworth, near Cleckheaton, though Charlotte renamed it Hallow's Mill and its owner became Robert Moore. Charlotte relates:

'Now Mr Moore loved machinery; he had risked the last of his capital on the purchase of these frames and shears which to-night had been expected; speculations most important to his interests depended on the results wrought by them; where were they?'

But the words 'We've smashed 'em!' soon rang in his ears.

The main ally of the mill owner is the Rev Matthewson Helston, uncle of Caroline Helston, and also the Rector of Briarfield (based on Birstall). The model for this inflexible cleric was the rather eccentric Vicar of Liversedge, the Rev Hammond Roberson, known to Mr Brontë. He built the church at Liversedge out of his own money and had many strong convictions, one being that during his time as vicar all the gravestones had to be rather small plain ones. There is a memorial window in his honour in the church he had built:

'To the glory of God, and in memory of the Rev Hammond Roberson MA Founder of this church in 1816, and its first incumbent who died 9th August, 1841, aged 84.'

Shirley is not all riots and unhappiness. Many pleasant episodes are set around Fieldhead in Briarfield, the home of the heroine Shirley Keeldar — intended by Charlotte to be a portrait of her sister Emily had she lived on with better health. One section of the novel tells how Caroline Helstone finds a new friend in Shirley. Along with her uncle she goes to call on Shirley, the owner of Fieldhead who has come to reside there for a time. Although Mr Helston is fond of Caroline, he often wishes she had more spirit and on this occasion rather unkindly informs her:

'She [Shirley] is rather a fine girl: she will teach you what it is to have a sprightly spirit, nothing lackadaisical about her.'

The author tells how Caroline quaked 'in spite of self-remembrance, as she and her uncle walked up the broad paved approach...'

The original of Fieldhead is Oakwell Hall, Birstall, now surrounded by a country park, though formerly much of this was farmland. In 1928, Oakwell Hall was in danger of being bought by an American and taken to the United States to be reconstructed there stone by stone. This was averted by Sir Norman Rae and Mr J E

Sharman, who bought it for public ownership and the building was opened as a museum. It is now in the care of Kirklees Museums Department and is open regularly all the year round.

The Red House in Gomersal is also in the care of the same department. One room was formerly devoted to the Brontës, but the building is currently undergoing structural repairs. This historic house, built in 1660, was well known to Charlotte as it was the home of her friend Mary Taylor, now buried in Gomersal churchyard. Charlotte visited her friend many times in the 1830's and portrayed her as Rose Yorke in *Shirley*. The Red House became the Yorke's family home, Briarmains:

'Briarmains stood near the highway, it is rather an old place and had been built ere the highway was cut...'

As well as the area around Gomersal, Charlotte knew nearby Birstall very well. She often stayed with her other friend Ellen Nussey who lived at a house there known as The Rydings. (Ellen is buried in Birstall churchyard.) Charlotte used the house as the basis for Mr Rochester's residence, Thornfield Hall, in *Jane Eyre* (1847). The Rydings is now in the grounds of a carpet factory, but can still be seen from near the road junction at the Smithies. In 1984 Kirklees Council secured a grade two preservation order for The Rydings. Ellen's old home can now never be demolished even though it is surrounded by industrial buildings. However, the firm that now owns the property have become keenly interested in its literary associations.

All the places mentioned which have literary connections with Charlotte and her friends are worth visiting for their own sakes, and there are many other places of interest in this part of Kirklees.

One of the district's other literary links is that with Herbert Knowles (1797-1817). At one time it was thought he was born at the Red House but research has shown, however, that the young poet was in fact born at Green Head near Huddersfield. The Knowles family were Gomersal wool merchants and James, Herbert's father, had moved to Huddersfield after his marriage to Elizabeth Phillips. It was here that Herbert (born on the 30th September 1797), Charles James and George were born. The eldest daughter Elizabeth was born in

June 1802 in London, since James Knowles carried on the family
business as a wool stapler in the capital. After his wife's death in
October 1803, James moved back to Gomersal. He too died in March
1805 at Hill Top House, the Knowles family residence, and was
buried in Heckmondwike.

After the death of his parents, the young Herbert came to the
impressive Elizabethan mansion of Pollard Hall in Gomersal to live
with his aunt and uncle, Sarah and William Burnley. He attended
school at Gomersal Hall before he and his brother Charles James were
sent to another school kept by a Mr Kempley.

The boy's life was changed when he moved back to London to live
with his uncle Phillips in Finsbury Square. Herbert was apprenticed
to a tobacco merchant, but hated the trade and ran away to enlist as
a soldier. An observant chaplain noticed that the young recruit
seemed unfitted for an army career and asked him if he could write.
On Knowles replying that he could, Mr Doyle requested him to
provide a sample of his work by eleven o'clock the next morning.
Herbert Knowles did just that — the sample being a hundred and
twenty verses about Canterbury Cathedral. This so impressed the
chaplain that the work came to the notice of Dr Andrews, the Dean
of Canterbury Cathedral and lecturer at St James's, Westminster,
who in turn asked a clergyman's widow travelling to North Yorkshire
if she could discover a good but reasonably priced school for Herbert,
The Rev James Tate, headmaster of Richmond Grammar School,
was so interested in the boy's welfare that he offered him schooling if
friends would provide £50 or so for books and clothing. Dr Andrews
supplied this amount, but four-fifths of it was unused and returned to
him after Herbert's early death.

Soon after, Knowles sent a poem of over 1,500 lines entitled
A Richmond Tale to the Poet Laureate Robert Southey, hoping to gain
advice on how to raise some money to pay his university fees. He must
have been an enterprising boy, for when Southey replied in October
1816 that he was unlikely to raise any money from writing, Knowles
wrote back asking the Poet Laureate to write to Mr Tate for a recommendation. His headmaster promised Southey: 'If you will answer for
his genius, I will make answer for his good conduct.'

Southey arranged for £30 per year for four years to be made available for Herbert Knowles. He himself was to supply £10 and the balance was to be given by Lord Spencer — who was so impressed by the young poet's work he named his own son Herbert — and a poet named Rogers. A sizarship was secured for Knowles at St John's College, Cambridge. Unhappily he died shortly after this, and is buried in the chapel yard in Heckmondwike. His tombstone is inscribed:

'Herbert Knowles. Died February 17th, 1817. His superior genius engaged for him the patronage of men eminent for rank, talents and learning, but the ardour of his mind destroyed the mortal tenements and he fell a victim to consumption at the age of 19 years.'

Today Herbert Knowles is best remembered for his verses *The Three Tabernacles: Stanzas on Richmond Churchyard,* written in October 1816.

Leeds is often regarded as the heartland of the West Riding. A tiny village of less than two hundred people at the time of Domesday, in the fourteenth century it was still much smaller than Pontefract. Even by the late fifteenth century it was referred to as being 'near Rothwell'. The eighteenth and nineteenth centuries were the time of great economic upheaval, and when Daniel Defoe visited Leeds at the turn of the eighteenth century he noted:

'Leeds is a large, wealthy and populous town, it stands on the north bank of the River Aire, or rather on both sides of the river, for there is a large suburb or part of the town on the south side of the river, and the whole is joined by a stately and prodigiously strong stone bridge, so large, and so wide, that formerly the cloth market was kept in neither part of the town, but on the very bridge itself.'

One of Leeds's earliest literary figures was a contemporary of Defoe's. William Congreve (1670-1729) was born in Bardsey, north-east of Leeds. He moved to Ireland while still young with his father, who commanded a garrison there. Educated in Ireland, and a fellow student of Jonathan Swift, he studied law in London for a while before achieving success with his dramatic comedy *The Old Bachelor* in 1693. He went on to write other plays now termed 'Restoration comedies', such as *The Double Dealer* (1694), *Love for Love* (1695) and *The Way of the World* (1700).

Nineteenth century literary visitors to Leeds commented mainly on the filth and squalor that plagued the area. As early as 1770 the poet Thomas Gray described the town as 'smoky and dingy', and Charles Dickens, who visited the Mechanics' Institute in 1847, said that Leeds was 'the beastliest place, one of the filthiest I know'. (Perhaps this view might have been due to a possibly unfavourable reception he received at the institute?) But around this time a Poet Laureate was born in the now picturesque suburb of Headingley, then little more than an outlying village.

Born into a Roman Catholic family, Alfred Austin (1835-1913) was intent on a legal career, though his father had been a wool-stapler. Educated at Stonyhurst School and graduating from London University in 1853, he was called to the bar in 1857 and served on the northern circuit. But when in 1858 he inherited money from his uncle, he abandoned his chosen profession, and became a full-time writer. At first he worked as a political journalist, and from 1883 he was co-editor of the *National Review* with W J Couthorpe, professor of poetry at Oxford, taking over full editorial control four years later.

During this time he also found opportunity to write poetry, and between 1871 and 1908 he wrote enough to fill twenty volumes. He believed himself to be a great poet, and was delighted when he was appointed Poet Laureate in 1896 after Tennyson's death. In this capacity he unveiled the Caedmon cross at Whitby, as has been mentioned. Yet he is probably best-remembered today for his non-fiction work *The Garden That I Love* (1894), based on his experiences of renovating his home near Ashford, Kent.

One of the classics of children's literature is Arthur Ransome's *Swallows and Amazons* (1931). It is not detracting from his strong links with the Lake District to include him in our literary survey of Yorkshire, for he was born in Leeds. His birthplace was a house on Woodhouse Lane (now demolished), close to his father's place of employment — Mr Ransome was professor of history at the Yorkshire College, which later became Leeds University. Arthur Ransome (1884-1967) knew Headingley well, for his family had moved to that part of Leeds when he was quite small. They lived in three different

houses, one being 3 St Chad's Villas near St Chad's Church. From
their home in Leeds, the family departed on long holidays to the Lake
District where young Arthur enjoyed fishing with his father. Closer
to home, one of his boyhood pleasures was to accompany him on
fishing trips on the River Wharfe.

His first school was run by a Miss Gledenning at nearby Adel,
though she lived in Headingley. He attended another local school
before boarding at Rugby, though he later returned home to become
a student of the Yorkshire College. His chosen subject was science, but
his mind constantly wandered onto literature — one of his greatest
pleasures at the time was to browse around the Leeds bookshops —
and though efforts to join the staff of a local newspaper failed, he was
granted an interview with the editor.

Like many northerners before and since, Ransome had to move
south in order to begin a career. He began as a office junior for the
publisher Grant Richards before going on to become a reporter for the
Daily News and *Manchester Guardian,* covering the Russian Revolution
for the former paper. (His second wife whom he married in 1924 had
once been Leon Trotsky's secretary.) It was as a writer of children's
fiction that he found fame, however, the series beginning with
Swallows and Amazons in 1931, describing the adventures of the Walker
and Blackett families in the Lake District. In all his work he followed
his own literary judgement that:

'All books are written to please and satisfy one person — their
author.'

Amongst modern authors who have written excellent fiction and
topographical books on Yorkshire is Lettice Cooper. She comes from
a family of whom many members were also authors and who have
connections with Leeds. For many years she lived in the Wetherby
area, but she now lives in London. Her first novel *The Lighted Room*
was published when she was only twenty years old. Others followed
including *National Provincial* (1938), revised by the author in 1968 and
again in 1987. This novel set in the West Riding between the wars has
as its heroine a successful journalist returning from London to live
with her crippled mother and younger brother. She obtains a job on

a local paper, but finds life humdrum at first. After attending a charity garden party, however, she becomes involved in a whirlpool of industrial strife and relationships which provides all the drama she desired. Apart from being a satisfying read, the novel also gives a realistic insight into industrial relations in the late 1930's.

A different novel altogether is *Snow and Roses,* published in 1976. This has a coalfield as its background, and is set around Garthwaite — supposedly about six miles from Doncaster. The plot centres on a miners' strike when Flora, a young Oxford lecturer, is visiting one of her best pupils, Nan (Anne) Coates, who was adopted as a baby by her aunt and uncle. Nan is a poet and has come back to her roots, finding inspiration there. As Flora approaches the mining community she comments to her companion:

'So this is Nan's home. It looks a strange breeding ground for a poet.'

This is not a disparagement of Nan's house, but of the environment. Her companion rightly replies:

'England seems able to breed them anywhere, or used to.'

As this book was being written a series of weekly monologues appeared on TV entitled *Talking Heads,* the work of Leeds-born Alan Bennett who now lives in the Dales. Each week viewers were invited to listen in on a section of life through the words and voiced thoughts of such characters as an inquisitive spinster and a vicar's wife. To anyone unfamiliar with this playwright's work, they show how he reveals an entertaining yet profound glimpse into human nature just through words.

Alan Bennett was born in 1934, and attended Leeds Modern School before graduating in modern history from Exeter College, Oxford. He found fame on stage in *Beyond the Fringe* in 1960, and later branched out into writing plays. Many of these are well-known to the theatre-going public and TV audiences for their unusual outlook and humour. Some have been published in book form, including *Forty Years and Other Plays* (1969), and these provide an opportunity to enjoy his subtle character-insight and wit. Recently Bennet has moved into films, with his screenplay of *A Private Function* (1984) — filmed in Ilkley

Alan Bennett.

The end cottage on Post Office Row, rented by Baring-Gould. Upstairs was the chapel, downstairs the school.

Stamp Office Yard in Westgate, Wakefield, where George Gissing and his mother moved to after Mr Gissing's death. An illustration by Henry Clarke for *Memories of Merry Wakefield* (1887) by Henry Clarkson.

and Bradford — and his adaptation of fellow playwright Joe Orton's biography *Prick Up Your Ears* (1987).

The West Riding does not owe all its literary heritage to past generations of writers. The year 1960 saw the publication of the novel *A Kind of Loving* by Stan Barstow. Born in 1928 in Ossett, south of Leeds, he was the son of a miner and educated at Ossett Grammar School. He then went to work in the drawing office of a local engineering firm, before switching to another part of the business.

When Barstow began to write his first novel, several young authors with working-class backgrounds like his own, such as Alan Sillitoe, John Braine and Hunslet-born Keith Waterhouse, were succeeding in a different type of fiction, writing novels with a strong regional background and populated by uncompromising, working-class characters. At first Barstow had begun his career by writing romantic fiction and then short stories for the BBC. The latter were often successful, especially one about a brass band, but he was on home ground there as his father was a keen bandsman. He then decided to write a novel, and sent it to a publisher. Surely his ideal Christmas present was when a letter arrived on Christmas Day accepting *A Kind of Loving* for publication.

Unlike some novelists, Stan Barstow decided to stay in his native Ossett, and he now lives in Goring House. His roots are in the town and its surroundings, as are many of his interests, In 1962 he finally became a full-time writer, and since then he has covered many areas, including TV. Other novels followed his first success, continuing his realistic portrayals of life in his native county. They include *Ask Me Tomorrow* (1962), *Joby* (1964), *The Watchers on the Shore* (1966) and *A Raging Calm* (1968). The main character in the latter novel is Tim Simphins, a local alderman who gets himself involved with a married woman while helping her with her domestic worries. Simphins tries to do his best for everybody, and provides an interesting character study. Barstow's writing always has that little extra something that makes it a genuine product of his landscape.

The York mystery plays may be the most famous of the remaining cycles, but Wakefield's mystery plays are also still performed, and

their origins and background are just as interesting as their older
counterparts. There are thirty-two plays in the Wakefield cycle, six of
the most learned written by the so-called 'Wakefield Master', which
like the York plays were intended to instil faith into a largely illiterate
audience. They are also known as the Towneley cycle, since they were
discovered in the library of Towneley Hall in Burnley. The cycle was
revived in 1980, and for the city of Wakefield's centenary celebrations
in 1988 a new version was put together by the Liverpool poet Adrian
Henri. Bradford-born Nick Ledgard played the part of Christ, and
Joe McAleese took the role of God. The cycle was staged in the
grounds of nearby Pontefract Castle, not only for its historical setting
but also because it helped to extend the centenary celebrations to other
parts of the Wakefield area.

Horbury, south-west of Wakefield, is proud of two associations; one
is that John Carr, the famous Yorkshire architect, was born in the little
township and built its fine parish church; the second is that a curate
of that parish in the last century was a well-known scholar, author,
folklorist, antiquarian and clergyman who turned his pen to virtually
every kind of writing.

Sabine Baring-Gould (1834-1924) was born at Exeter in Devon,
and spent much of his youth travelling through Europe with his
parents. Much of his later life was spent as parson and squire of Lew
Trenchard in his native county, but inbetween he led a fascinating
double career as a prolific author and clergyman in Yorkshire,
neglecting neither side of his work.

After studying classics at Cambridge, he became a teacher for a
time before deciding to become a clergyman. He was ordained deacon
by Bishop Bickersteth in Ripon Cathedral in 1864, and priest the
following year. At the time of his ordination as deacon, Horbury's
vicar was Canon John Sharp. Baring-Gould went to this small West
Riding township as Sharp's curate, but the main part of his work was
in the rather rough area around Horbury Bridge. Its population
consisted largely of miners and textile workers, and the new curate's
task was to strengthen the little mission church. Baring-Gould rented
the end cottage on Post Office Row, which is now the post office. He

described it as 'two doors from the Horse and Jockey'. Services and meetings were held in the upper room, and the kitchen downstairs was turned into a tiny school. The present small church of Horbury Bridge was built much later, and consecrated on the 15th November 1883 to coincide with the jubilee of the Rev John Sharp as Vicar of Horbury.

When Baring-Gould was curate the lads of the area tried to disrupt his services or meetings by throwing stones at the upstairs window. The curate could be classed as a kind of Victorian 'militant Christian' — at least he was determined that such behaviour was not going to interfere with his ministry. So he would often as not dash downstairs, seize the ringleader of the gang and march him up to become a chorister there and then. After this had happened a few times, he had little more trouble with vandalism. Apart from the popular services enjoyed by many of the hamlet's inhabitants and his fifty-odd Sunday school pupils constantly demanding a story after school, Baring-Gould was kept extremely busy with all his parish activities. (He was often so tired after his day's work that he slept in the upper room instead of returning to the vicarage.) He began a regular savings bank for the local workers, and started 'penny readings' where the audience paid one penny to listen to an improving novel or edifying book. Baring-Gould was a keen advocate of these 'penny readings' but he did suffer some disillusionment when he ventured to include short extracts from Shakespeare's works in his programme. His audiences dwindled until he resumed readings from what to them were extracts from more interesting works.

It soon became evident that the tiny cottage was far too small, so Baring-Gould arranged for the purchase of some land on which was built a parish hall — which still stands — the building materials being provided free by a local quarry owner.

His own literary career had begun in 1857 before he became a clergyman with the publication of *Path of the Just,* and in 1863 he wrote *Ireland: Its Scenes and Sagas.* Though for the greater part of his life he had at least two careers at any one time, he once commented:

'It is a change of work rather than a cessation from work which refreshes the mental powers.'

Eccentric people and their habits delighted him, and he collected information about many Yorkshire people who came into this category.

Accounts of some of these are included in his *Yorkshire Oddities* (1874). Baring-Gould had a great affection for the county and its people, and in his preface he wrote:

'No other county produces so much originality — and that originality, when carried to excess, is eccentricity.

I look back with the greatest pleasure to the kindness and hospitality I met with in Yorkshire, where I spent some of the happiest years of my life. I venture to offer this collection...as a humble contribution to the annals of the greatest, not perhaps only in extent, of our English counties...'

Other non-fiction works written by this industrious clergyman, covering topography, folklore and legend, are also becoming more popular in modern times.

He made Horbury world-famous during his two year stay as it was here that he wrote the hymn *Onward Christian Soldiers* for his Horbury Bridge scholars to sing as they marched up the hill to meet the children from the parish church on Whit Monday 1865. As is often the case — it happened with Francis Lyte's *Abide With Me* — doubts have been cast that Baring-Gould had actually written the hymn words specifically for the procession. A letter in possession of Horbury Bridge Church dated April 1918 proves, however, that the hymn was actually written for the event in question. It was from a man who had lived at Standbridge House, Horbury, at the time of the procession, and had actually taken part.

Baring-Gould left Horbury in 1866 to become Vicar of Dalton in the North Riding, where he remained until 1871 when the Prime Minister, Mr Gladstone, offered him the living of East Mersea in Essex. He had returned briefly to Horbury in May 1868 in order to marry Grace Taylor, a working-class girl whom, in the best Victorian novel tradition, he had had specially educated for her new position, and she eventually bore him fifteen children.

He portrayed the parish of his first curacy in two of his novels,

Through Fire and Flame (1868) and *The Pennycumquicks*, and it is believed that Annis, the mill girl heroine of the former novel, is based on his wife. These and many of his other novels were intended to provide interesting books for a generation that had only recently learned to read and write, but today provide a look at life during those times. Altogether Baring-Gould wrote dozens of books, numerous religious works and other non-fiction, and even wrote a book about ghosts published in 1904.

In 1981 he moved to Lew Trenchard in Devon, and later became its squire. There he undertook invaluable research into old folk songs and other customs associated with the West Country. He died on the 7th January 1924, leaving to literature, folklore and religion a veritable treasure-trove of research and authorship.

When Baring-Gould's first book was published in 1857, a little boy was born in Wakefield who was to become a famous novelist. George Robert Gissing (1857-1903) was born in a house up Thompson's Yard, behind his father's chemist's shop. Until recently a tablet was fixed to the shop formerly owned by his father, Thomas Walter Gissing, at 30 Westgate. It read:

'This tablet was erected to commemorate the birthplace of George Robert Gissing (1857-1903), Novelist and Man of Letters.'

That tablet is now outside his Georgian birthplace, which is in the care of The Gissing Trust, set up in 1979. Its secretary and Gissing expert is Mr Clifford Brook JP, and over the last twenty years Mr Brook's keen interest in the novelist has resulted in an increased amount of research into his life, work and the places associated with him, especially in his home town. Mr Brooke has arranged walks in the area, intended for anyone who wished to learn more about Gissing's local associations. These are especially around the St John's area, Back Lane — young George attended a school here which can still be seen — and the Westgate district of the city.

His father, Thomas Gissing, was a Suffolk man who bought what was at that time the largest chemist's shop in Wakefield from a Mr Hick. He was a keen botanist and published books on the ferns found around Wakefield. In 1896, twenty-six years after his father's death,

George was delighted to see his father's name included in the index of British botanists in the British Museum. In addition, Thomas was also in charge of the library in the local Mechanics' Institute along Wood Street; the building now houses the Wakefield Museum, but still bears the inscription of its former usage. According to the novelist H G Wells, who later became a friend of his, Gissing could always cheer himself up by remembering the sights and smells of the chemist's shop — especially camphor — and his father's constant encouragement.

Thomas Gissing died suddenly in 1870 and the pleasant life in the gracious house ended abruptly. Mrs Gissing was left badly off financially and the family moved to a small house in Stamp Office Yard, also in Westgate, but in a poorer part of that area. Later Mrs Gissing moved again to St Catherine's Villas, now part of a large hotel but previously known as Stoneleigh Terrace. George and his two brothers were sent as boarders to Linton Grove Quaker School at Alderley Edge in Cheshire. There he worked hard and in a letter to his mother tells her he has sat for a science examination, going on to say that he is working:

'...in earnest for my great exam, the Oxford. If I pass I don't care [about the hard work he has done]...This is in about three weeks, so that I have but very little time...how time does go. I never knew a half go so quickly in my life, I suppose it is having so many exams. If I pass all I go up for, I shall have passed five this half.'

Always in his mind was the desire to fulfil his late father's hopes for him. He succeeded in this when, at fifteen years old, he won a free place to Owen's College, Manchester. Here he achieved further honours, before he wrecked his scholastic career by pilfering to help a girl of low reputation whom he loved. His friends packed him off to America, and on his return he set out to make a living as a novelist. His novel *Workers of the Dawn,* published in 1880 when he was only twenty-three, was followed by other works such as *The Unclassed* (1884), *New Grub Street* (1891) and *Born in Exile* (1892).

Something of the bitter struggles he experienced as a writer are related in *The Private Papers of Henry Ryecroft* (1903), based partly on the time he spent in Exeter between 1881 and 1883. (He also wrote two novels set in the area, and it is interesting to speculate whether he ever met Baring-Gould, the former curate of Horbury now resident at nearby Lew Trenchard.) Gissing believed that this semi-autobiographical story of a man 'of independent and scornful outlook, who had suffered much from defeated ambition' was the 'best thing' he had done, and it was certainly the book that brought him more fame and money than any other thing he had written. He described it as:

'...the thing most likely to last when all my other futile work has followed my futile life.'

He was too pessimistic; his novels are still read, and there has recently been a resurgence of interest in his work.

What can be called his 'Wakefield novel', *A Life's Morning* (1888), was one of his earlier efforts. The plot centres around Emily Hood, governess to a family in the south. The son, Wilfrid, falls in love with her, but the marriage is bitterly opposed by his aunt, and only tolerated if held at some future date by the father of Wilfrid. In order to escape from her dilemma, Emily returns to her home town of Dunfield (Wakefield). However her parents are worse off financially than she had imagined, and her father is an unsuccessful businessman who has been compelled to take work as a poorly paid clerk in the offices of a local manufacturer, a complex character called Richard Dagworthy.

Dagworthy sees Emily when she and her father are taking a walk over a stretch of open countryside near the town (this is in reality Heath Common). He falls in love with her and soon afterwards asks her to marry him. She refuses, so he concocts a plot which involves a ten pound note hidden in one of his office ledgers. Mr Hood finds it, removes it with every intention of giving it to his employer as soon as he can find him, but is sent on an errand to a neighbouring city (Leeds) before he can do so. His hat blows away and he dare not keep the appointment without headgear, so he purchases a new hat using some of the ten pound note, with every intention of paying it back. Then he meets an old friend and borrows more of the money to help him and also stand him a decent meal, for the man is half-starving.

Of course the note has been planted by Dagworthy in the first place so that he can blackmail Emily into marrying him. Happily he fails and — though Mr Hood commits suicide — Wilfrid comes to the rescue of his sweetheart, they are married and all ends happily. Strangely enough Gissing did not want a happy ending — to him it seemed false. But he had to change the original ending to please his publisher and 'the market', since as usual he badly needed the money. But that is probably why his insight into the struggles of his characters is so realistic; he knew what their lives were really like since he had experienced something of their predicaments himself.

Although Wakefield residents of the last century were not too pleased with Gissing's bleak view of their town, their descendants lived to be proud of their nineteenth century novelist whose books are now rightly regarded as classics.

As soon as David Storey published his first book he started to collect awards and prizes of one sort or another. The book in question, *This Sporting Life,* was published in 1960 and won the prestigious Macmillan Fiction Award of America. Born in 1933, he was the third son of a miner in one of the local pits. He went to school at Queen Elizabeth Grammar School in Wakefield, then on to the Slade School of Fine Art in London. He became a teacher for a time, as well as a farm worker and a professional rugby league player. His experiences in the latter profession are brought out in his first novel.

This Sporting Life is an account of Arthur Machin, a headstrong young man who works in an engineering firm but who also has the potential to become a great rugby league player for his local team, and perhaps beyond. Mr Weaver, the managing director of his firm, is also one of the top men of the local rugby league club, and so Arthur soon finds himself involved with him in many different ways. Arthur's life is further complicated by the fact that he becomes involved in a relationship with his landlady, whose husband's death at the engineering works was partly due to his own carelessness.

The detail in the story is evident to anyone familiar with the rugby league game. Even to those not so well informed, there are many interesting insights as to how Arthur's new-found affluence affects his behaviour. One of the most telling incidents is at a 'country club'-type restaurant one weekend when Arthur takes his landlady and her children out for the day in his big new car. Before they arrive at the luxurious restaurant — which has a cafe to one side for more proletarian customers — Arthur has to rescue the little daughter from the dangerous stepping stones in a riverside beauty spot. In the process he gets his feet very wet, and changes into his spare pair of football boots he keeps in the car. Wearing these, he marches his little party not into the cafe but the restaurant, and takes his place at a table. The silent horror of the well-heeled middle-class people enjoying their lunch is enhanced when they notice his boots, and the waiter also looks as if he would like to direct them to another part of the establishment. But Arthur, confident in his wealth, insists on having the best for his party. His guests are not so comfortable, however, and they are all glad when they escape back to his large car. Storey successfully illuminates the problems that have to be faced by ambitious working-class men today as they move into a different environment.

David Storey's other novels were greeted with similar acclaim. *Flight into Camden* (1966) was granted the Somerset Maugham Award and the John Llewellyn Memorial Prize, and *Saville,* set in a South Yorkshire mining town and a great favourite with northern readers, won the Booker Prize in 1976. All his work as a novelist, and latterly as dramatist, have shown him to be a convincing portrayer of modern northern life.

The Poet Laureate Sir John Betjeman observed in 1980 that Wakefield did not make the most of itself. Probably he held the same opinion about nearby historic Pontefract. He visited 'Ponty' for the first time in 1970, but it had already been the setting of one of his most famous poems, *The Liquorice Fields of Pontefract,* several years before. After visiting the town he commented:

'I really like Ponty — its got lots of good stuff in it.'

As might be expected, he has not been the only literary visitor to Pontefract to mention liquorice. Celia Fiennes had learned something about this plant and its uses in the eighteenth century when she noted:

'The gardens are all filled with it and anybody [who has a garden] grows it.'

As we have seen, Celia did not particularly delve into history of the places she visited, but was content with taking a general interest in their appearance. She described 'Pomfret' — its old name — as a place of:

'...neate buildings and the streets well pitch'd and broad, the houses well built and look more stately than any in York, only it's not the tenth part as bigg; it's a neate little town.'

In fact she was most enthusiastic about Pontefract, and rather reluctant to leave. Unfortunately she was unable to obtain accommodation at Hemsworth 'or two miles further on' (was this historic Ackworth?). Then a Mr Ferrer, a clergyman who had been Vicar of All Saints in Pontefract until deprived of his living in 1661, gave Celia and her companions hospitality. From his home they travelled south to Rotherham, which Celia thought of as a good, well-built market town:

'The church stands high in the middle of the town and looks finely, it's all stone and carved very well on the outside.'

With past comments about an impressive church that used to be in a West Riding town, but is now classed as being in South Yorkshire, our literary journey moves on to that 'new' part of the county.

South Yorkshire

As South Yorkshire came into existence only after 1974 it may seem a little strange in this journey round the county to consider it separately from the old West Riding, but it has enough famous literary forebears for a chronological survey of its own.

One of the earliest writers to have a connection with South Yorkshire was Geoffrey Chaucer (1343-1400). As a boy he was believed to have been in the service of Elizabeth, Countess of Ulster, the then owner of Hatfield Manor, north-east of Doncaster. However, there seems to be no trace of any early poems or writings which make firm the association with the London-born writer who later penned the celebrated *Canterbury Tales*.

Although Epworth is now situated in South Humberside, its Doncaster postal address is a reminder of its links with this part of Yorkshire, and as the Wesleys lived in Epworth Old Rectory it seems fitting to include something about them in this book. John Wesley (1703-1791) is especially associated with the county, as his *Journal* reveals. The 1988 celebrations to mark the 250th anniversary of his conversion brought his life and work even more into prominence.

In 1709 a terrible fire broke out in the Wesleys' home and six year old John was almost burnt to death. His own presence of mind is reputed to have saved his life, for it is told how he dragged a piece of furniture to the window of the second floor room where he was trapped so that the villagers could see him and rescue him. In later life he often described himself as 'a brand plucked from the burning', and believed that he had been saved for some great purpose. The work he did throughout his life illustrates that purpose. Today Epworth Old Rectory is a conference centre and museum, opened in 1957 by the World-Wide Methodist Church.

The small village of Aston, east of Sheffield, had a new rector in 1754, the Rev William Mason (1725-1797). No doubt none of his new parishioners would have imagined that one of the most famous poems in the English language would be discussed by its author and his friend in the pleasant summerhouse of the rectory opposite the church, which Mason rebuilt and is now known as the Old Rectory. (This is now a private residence.) Soon after arriving in Aston, Mrs Mason died and the reverend was always delighted when his friend Thomas Gray (1716-1771) visited him. Gray wrote that 'Skroddles', his nickname for Mason, had found 'an Elysium amongst the coal pits'. Together they visited the local landmarks such as Roche Abbey.

Educated at Eton and Oxford, Mason had become a great friend of Gray's at university, where they were both keenly interested in the study and writing of poetry. Mason was also a playwright: his *Elfrida* (1752) and *Caractacus* (1759) were performed in York after first appearing in Dublin and London respectively. The 1772 performance of *Elfrida* was for the benefit of Tate Williamson, York Theatre Royal's manager and producer for thirty-seven years. (At the time Mason was prebendary at York Minster.)

Thomas Gray's life was entirely different from Mason's, quietly passed at Cambridge and in writing poetry. He travelled widely, especially in England, writing down his impressions in his journals and letters. It was while staying with his aunt at Stoke Poges in Buckinghamshire that he wrote *Elegy Written in a Country Churchyard*. Gray did not intend to publish it, though he discussed some of the verses with Mason and even omitted one at his friend's behest. Eventually the poem was published, and the quiet, nervous Gray became known as its author. In 1757 he was offered the Poet Laureateship, but he refused as he preferred his quiet life.

After Gray's death, Mason became his literary executor, published a life of him, edited his letters and poems and wrote the poet's epitaph for his tomb in Westminster Abbey.

Francis Fawkes (1721-1777), a member of a branch of the famous Fawkes family, was born at Warmsworth near Doncaster, where his father was rector. Declining to enter the church, Fawkes spent much of his time translating the classics. He did, however, write a number of poems, including *Bramham Park* (1745), whose title is self-explanatory; *Partridge Shooting* (1767), indicating his love of field sports; and he also tried his hand at lighter verse, including one entitled *The Brown Jug.*

A different type of poet althogether was Ebenezer Elliott (1781-1849). One of eleven children, he was born in Mexborough near Rotherham, where his father owned the New Foundry. Ebenezer was educated at Penistone Grammar School and soon developed a love of literature, fostered by a legacy of books left to him by a neighbouring clergyman.

The fact that he married a wealthy young lady helped to set him up in business as owner of an ironworks. (His wife's relations also stood by him financially in some of his business transactions.) After becoming an ironmaster in Sheffield in 1821 — retiring some twenty-one years later — he managed even while running a business to write many poems. Today he is probably best remembered for the poems that earned him the name of the 'Corn Law Rhymer'. These poems were sparked off by the increased price of bread, the poor man's staple diet, and Elliott was genuinely distressed by the misery and want these laws caused.

Yet his other poems are worth remembering for the vivid descriptions of some of the beautiful scenery around his native area. Some of this still exists not far from the busy industrial centres. At least one of his poems would find favour with modern conservationists, as he wrote how the town was usurping the country:

> 'But such he dreads the
> Town's distracting maze
> Where all in lies is full of change and where
> New streets invade the country and he strays
> Lost in strange paths, still seeking and in vain
> For ancient landmarks of the lowly lane
> Whereof he played Crusoe as a boy.'

His first major poem *The Vernal*, was written when he was only seventeen years old. Subjects crowded into his brain as he took long walks around South Yorkshire, especially the areas around Sheffield and Rotherham. The beautiful Rivelin Valley can be reached through Walkley, and even though the first part has the mark of industry there are still many lovely areas to explore. Elliott wrote in *Farewell to Rivelin:*

> 'Beautiful river, goldenly shining,
> Where, with the vistas, woodlands are binding...
> Rivelin wildest! Do I not love thee?'

One of his best known nature poems is *The Yews of Maltby,* and his travels often took him further afield in Yorkshire, resulting in work on Fountains Abbey and Wharfedale. Sometimes he chose rather doleful subjects, such as his poet's prayer:

> 'Almighty father, let thy lowly child
> Strong in his love of truth be wisely bold —
> A portrait laid by sycophants reviled.
> Help his line usually and not die old,
> Let poor men's children pleased to read his lays,
> Love for his sake the scenes where he hath been;
> And, when he ends his pilgrimage of days,
> Let him be buried where the grass is green.'

He even wrote a poem about the sculptor Sir Francis Chantrey, who had delivered milk when a boy near where Elliott lived.

Around 1840 he came into contact with the poet and playwright John Watkins, who at the time of their first correspondence lived at Aislaby near Whitby. Elliott was planning his retirement, and asked Watkins to learn more about a property that might be suitable near Whitby. By the time the enquiries had been made, Elliott had decided to stay in his own part of Yorkshire. On the 11th January 1841, he wrote to Watkins to tell him that he had:

> '...just contracted for the building of a humble cottage of about eight rooms, on ten acres of bad land at Great Houghton.'

He added:

> 'There is a weekly carrier from Pontefract and Rotherham.'

John Watkins left Whitby and moved south. Several years later he decided:

A view of the Rivelin Valley so beloved by Ebenezer Elliott. Sketch by Mr
C Thompson in the *Illustrated Guide to Sheffield* (1862) by Pawson
and Brailsford.

Conisbrough Castle

An engraving of Rotherham's parish church. Taken from John Guest's
Relics and Records of Men, Manufacturers at or in the Neighbourhood of Rotherham
(1866).

'I was desirous of visiting the most interesting relic of antiquity in Yorkshire, or in England, — the ruins of Conisbrough Castle. Miss Elliott accompanied me.'

This could not have been their first meeting, for Watkins proposed marriage to Fanny Elliott on the outing. Her father was delighted, but confessed to Watkins that he was seriously ill and unlikely to recover, though his daughter did not know this. His last verse was:

> 'When from my eyes earth's lifeful throng
> Has passed away, no more to be
> The autumn primrose, Robin's song
> Return to me.'

He chose to be buried in the churchyard in Darfield, south-east of Barnsley, because John and Fanny were married at the church.

Growing up in Edinburgh at the time that Elliott was born was a ten year old boy who would become one of the greatest authors of historical fiction. Walter Scott (1771-1832), after 1820 Sir Walter, is one writer who has made the past live again for readers of all ages.

Yet not all his life's work was spent as an author. Early in his life he became a law clerk, was eventually appointed sherriff-deputy at Selkirk and also clerk of the sessions in Edinburgh. His work took him to many parts of Scotland, and later his writing brought him to England. Never content with accepting the facts and scenes for his books at second hand, he enjoyed nothing more than setting out on explorations to research the backgrounds for himself, visiting each place he described in his novels and inspecting almost every beauty spot and landmark mentioned in his writings.

His first writing successes came with ballads, including *Marmion* (1808), *The Lady of the Lake* (1810) and *Rokeby* (1813). Then came his 'Waverley' series of novels, named after the first romance he wrote under that title. He was a well-established novelist by the time he wrote one of his most famous works, based in Yorkshire.

On his journeys round the country he kept a keen eye on the landscape through which he was travelling. Once while passing through South Yorkshire he noticed a fine old castle, and in December

1811 he wrote to his friend John Morritt of Rokeby Park, Teesdale, stating:

'I once flew past in small mail coach a castle with its round tower and flying buttresses — had a most romantic effect in the morning dawn.'

As usual his friend supplied the answer to its identity. Walter Scott came to South Yorkshire to explore the area round the ancient town of Conisbrough and its nearby castle. Even before the Civil War this castle had been neglected so much that neither the Parliamentary forces nor the Royalist armies bothered to attack it, as they did so many better-preserved castles. When Walter Scott came to write *Ivanhoe* (1819) he began the novel with a description of the countryside around the castle:

'In that pleasant district of Merry England which is watered by the River Don there extended in ancient times a large forest covering a greater part of the beautiful hills and valleys which lie between Sheffield and the pleasant town of Doncaster.'

Strangely enough that opening did not find favour with one boy. William Watson, born in Burley-in-Wharfedale, asked his schoolmaster if there was any worse opening to a book 'known to exist'. Whatever young Watson thought of the opening, other readers enjoyed the story and continue to do so to this day.

After collecting his background material the author is reputed to have stayed for three nights at Sprotborough, just north of Doncaster. In 1865 the then rector of that parish, the Rev Scott F Suttees, wrote to T S B Eastwood, president of the Rotherham Literary and Scientific Society stating:

'Mr Wood, who is now about sixty years old, and is Sir Joseph Copley's steward married the daughter of Mr B Neville who kept the public-house called the Sprotborough Boathouse. Mr Wood had heard that Sir Walter Scott had stayed there; and that there is an armchair called "Sir Walter's Chair".'

Another clue is that the then baronet Sir Joseph Copley revealed that his father had told him that Scott had visited Sprotborough before he wrote *Ivanhoe*.

Although parts of *Ivanhoe* are set in other places — for example Prince John holds a feast for his supporters at York Castle, and the character of Isaac the Jew of York lives in Castlegate in that same city — the area around Conisbrough is rightly regarded as Ivanhoe country. In the novel the castle is the home of Athelstane; nearby Rotherham became Rotherwood; and Kirk Sandal, Barnaby Dun, Norton and Ashton are all featured.

If Sir Walter Scott did write part of his historical romance while staying at the Boathouse, it is unlikely the section would be altered in any way. According to Scott's son-in-law Lockhart, the author of *The Life of Sir Walter Scott*, very rarely did Sir Walter ever rewrite his work before sending it to the publishers. The same author records how *Ivanhoe* was one of the very few novels that Scott did not write out entirely in his own hand — instead he dictated some parts of it to one of the two men he occasionally employed as secretaries. Originally it had been Scott's intention to have this particular novel issued as if it had been written by someone else, but at the last minute the publisher, Constable, remonstrated against the scheme.

The old town of Conisbrough is a pleasant place in itself, with many interesting old buildings, but it is the twelfth century castle that visitors come to see. It was erected on land given by William the Conqueror, but it was Hemoline Plantagenet, the half-brother of Henry II, who had the keep erected on the site and the surrounding parts of the castle. The view from the castle is industrial, but the surrounding grounds remain pastoral with the river Don flowing close by. Over the years more and more people have visited Conisbrough because they had read *Ivanhoe* and wanted to explore the setting. (This is still possible today, since the castle is now part of English Heritage.) Conisbrough Castle provided Scott with a good background for an excellent story. But Scott did much more — he made the castle famous to readers the world over.

It is unlikely that Anthony Trollope (1815-1882) would have worried about either *Ivanhoe* or Conisbrough Castle on his journey to Rotherham. His mission was marriage to Rose Heseltine, daughter of a Rotherham banker. The two had met in Ireland where the future novelist was a post office surveyor. It was a turning point in Trollope's life. Up until then he had endured all kinds of frustrations and hindrances. According to some reports he was a poor scholar, and his childhood was very unhappy — both at school and at home — for his father was often in financial difficulties. His mother Frances Trollope later became a well-known novelist, and her work was eagerly read both in Britain and America; it was her success that revived the family fortunes.

In 1834 Anthony Trollope applied for the position of clerk in the General Post Office in London. (Years later he based the examination endured by Charley Taylor in *The Three Clerks* on his own experiences.) He was appointed and for seven years was most unhappily employed. Then in 1841 came the chance to apply for the position of surveyor in Ireland. He was amazed when he was given the job — but later he learned that no-one else had applied! It turned out to be a very fortunate move for him, not only was he happier in Ireland than he had ever been before in his life but he also met his future wife who was staying at Kingston near Dublin. After a few years' delay they were married at Holy Trinity Parish Church in Rotherham on the 11th June 1844. The wedding was a simple affair — none of the bridegroom's family attended — but it was the start of over forty years of happy marriage. In his *Autobiography* (1883) he wrote:

'I ought to name that happy day as the commencement of my better life, rather than the day on which I landed in Ireland. My marriage was like the marriage of other people and of no special interest to anyone except my wife and me.

It took place at Rotherham in Yorkshire. We were not rich, having about £400 a year on which to live.'

When he came to write his novels he found his wife a great help, though she is rarely mentioned in any accounts of his second career. For years she acted as his secretary, making excellent copies of his manuscripts for the publishers. This work was not spasmodic, for Trollope went to his writing table most methodically every morning. He began his day's stint by reading what he had written the day before, which he estimated took him about half an hour. He then set himself to write a certain number of words, whether he felt like it or not. This very regularity caused his work to fall from favour with some people when his *Autobiography* was published after his death. It was seen as too commercial an attitude for those Victorians who thought that all writers should sit gazing into space until inspiration decided to appear — or not as the case may be.

His first books, *The Mackdermots of Ballycloran* (1847) and *The Kellys and the O'Kells* (1848), were not very successful. Real success came with *The Warden* in 1855, the first of the remarkable 'Barchester' novels. Others followed including *Barchester Towers* (1857) with the introduction of that formidable female, the bishop's wife Mrs Proudie. He once heard some fellow clubman complaining about her, and went home and is said to have 'killed her off'. Later, however, he revived her for another novel.

Not all Trollope's ambitions were fulfilled by his literary work. In 1868 he decided to stand as a Parliamentary candidate for Beverley in the old East Riding. Even when he was a post office clerk he had informed his uncle that he would like to be an MP one day. His uncle had scoffed at the very idea of his nephew ever achieving his ambition. Trollope earnestly believed it should be the wish of all patriotic Englishmen to be returned to Parliament, and decided that to serve one's country without payment 'is the greatest work that a man can do'.

He came to stand for Beverley by way of Essex, so to speak, for he was first offered the chance to stand for the latter place in 1867, but the expected vacancy did not arise. After Disraeli's Reform Bill of 1867, Trollope became candidate for Beverley. He had no happy recollections of the town, nor of his endeavours. At first nothing dampened his spirits, but gradually his experiences and the dismal attitude of his agent began to affect his hopes. The agent told him:

'You won't get in. I don't suppose you expect it, but there is a fine career open to you. You will spend £1,000 and lose the election. Then you will petition and spend another £1,000. You will throw out the elected member. There will be a commission and the borough will be disfranchised. For a beginner such as you are, that will be a great success.'

At that time elections were marred by many illegal practices, as portrayed in many Victorian novels.

Trollope spent his time canvassing for votes in extremely rainy weather. He did not like the evening meetings either, stating:

'At night, every night, I had to speak somewhere, which was bad; and had to listen to the speaking of others, which was worse...'

Honest to the core, Trollope later described that fortnight of his campaign as the 'most wretched fortnight of my manhood'. He came at the bottom of the poll. Later, however, there was some conflict about the election with the result that the winning candidate did not hold his seat for long. Trollope felt he had spent his time and money in a good cause, for it had ended the corrupt system of boroughs in one town at least.

One of the most influential critics and authors on art and literature during the last century was John Ruskin (1819-1900), who had close links with many parts of Yorkshire. One of his favourite places was Sheffield, not for its beauty — parts of the city were scarred by iron-works and the shops of the 'little mesters', the small one-man cutlery businesses — but because it afforded him an oppportunity to put forward some of his ideas on craftsmanship and art, and also to share his knowledge and possessions with appreciative working men whom he admired.

John Ruskin, born in Surrey the son of a wealthy wine-merchant, had a very sheltered childhood, but one in which he was often taken abroad by his parents. This rapidly fostered his appreciation of beautiful buildings, pictures, art and great books. When he grew up he wanted to share those experiences and found that South Yorkshire, especially Sheffield and its Guild of St George (craftsmen and workers in the city with a keen appreciation of their skills), provided him with an opportunity to do so.

He admired the ironworkers and believed their characteristics were old English in temperament. He tried to instil in them an understanding of what he saw as the heroic and feudal ideals, as opposed to the oppressive and fiercely competitive nature of nineteenth century industrial Britain. In 1876 Ruskin purchased eleven acres of land at

John Ruskin.

The Ruskin Gallery

Abbeydale on behalf of the guild. He wanted to keep the advance of heavy industry from at least one part of Sheffield, and said:

'We will try and make some small piece of English ground beautiful, peaceful and fruitful. We shall have no steam engines upon it, and no railroads.'

The land was at first used to grow fruit and vegetables, and is now the Abbeydale Industrial Hamlet, visited by hundreds of people each year.

Ruskin's life and work is remembered in Sheffield itself at the Ruskin Gallery on Norfolk Street, not far from the Crucible Theatre. This building is the successor to the first small museum opened at Walkley by the Guild of St George. Ruskin offered them many books and paintings from his own vast collection. He wrote from his home, Brantwood in Cumbria, that what was required was 'a room with good light' in which to display the exhibits.

Eventually the Ruskin Museum moved to Meerbrook Park, purchased by the city of Sheffield and offered to Ruskin and the guild. Situated in forty acres of fine grounds, the museum was very popular with local people. The collection remained at Meerbrook Park until 1953 when it was housed on loan to Reading University; it has since returned to its home city of Sheffield in recent years.

Like many of the people who have been covered in this survey, Ruskin's books encourage more enquiries in a county rich in literature. One area of interest often leads to another in a journey such as this, not only in the search for the background to authors' lives but also how the books themselves are a revealing portrayal of the people and times of Yorkshire.

It is these links between the past and present, some of which I hope have been illuminated in the previous pages, that can bring past writers' words to life. It is that which makes this kind of literary survey so rewarding and interesting.

Places to Visit

TREASURER'S HOUSE
Chapter House Street
York

Tel (0904) 24247

Open: 1st April to 31st October, every day except Fridays, 10.30am to 5.30pm. Last admission 4.30pm.

ST WILLIAM'S COLLEGE
College Street
York

Tel (0904) 37134

Open: All the year round.

CASTLE HOWARD
Nr Malton

Tel (065 384) 333

Open: Every day from 25th March to 31st September, 11am to 4.30pm.

SHANDY HALL
Coxwold
Nr York

Tel (034 76) 465

Open: At present during the summer on Wednesday afternoons, or by previous arrangement. The gardens are also open at certain times in connection with the National Gardens Scheme for Yorkshire.

BYLAND ABBEY
Coxwold
Nr York

Tel (034 76) 614

Open: Mid-March to mid-October, Monday to Saturday 9.30am to 6.30pm, Sundays 2pm to 6pm. Mid-October to mid-March, Monday to Saturday 9.30am to 4pm, Sundays 2pm to 4pm.

WOOD END MUSEUM
The Crescent
Scarborough

Tel (0723) 367326

Open: Tuesday to Saturday 10am to 1pm, 2pm to 5pm. From Spring Bank Holiday to the end of September, Sunday 2pm to 5pm. Closed Mondays, also Good Friday, 24th and 25th December and 1st January.

STEPHEN JOSEPH THEATRE-IN-THE-ROUND
Valley Bridge Parade
Scarborough

Tel (0723) 370540

Details of the programme from the theatre.

WHITBY ABBEY
Whitby

Tel (0947) 603568

Open: March to October, Monday to Saturday 9.30am to 6.30pm, Sunday 2pm to 4.30pm. October to March, Monday to Saturday 9.30am to 4pm, Sunday 2pm to 4.30pm. Also open from 9.30am on Sunday from 1st April to 30th September.

WHITBY MUSEUM
Pannett Park
Whitby

Tel (0947) 602908

Open: May to September, Monday to Saturday 9.30am to 1.30pm, Sunday 2pm to 5pm. October to April, Monday, Tuesday, Thursday and Friday 10.30am to 1pm, Wednesday and Saturday 10.30am to 4pm, Sunday 2pm to 4pm.

BOLTON CASTLE
Leyburn
North Yorkshire

Tel (0969) 23981

Open: Every day from March to October.

FOUNTAINS ABBEY
Nr Ripon

Tel (076 586) 333

Open: Abbey and grounds open from 10am all the year round except the 24th and 25th December. Closing time varies with the time of year.

SKIPTON CASTLE
Skipton

Tel (0756) 2442

Open: Daily with the exception of the 25th December and Good Friday.

MALHAM TARN FIELD CENTRE
Malham
Nr Settle

Tel (072 93) 331

Open: Existing to promote 'environmental understanding for all', visitors can stay at the centre and courses are arranged for parties and family groups.

BRONTË PARSONAGE MUSEUM
Church Street
Haworth

Tel (0535) 42323

Open: Daily between 11am and 4.30pm from October to March, 11am to 5.30pm April to September. Closed from the 1st to 21st February and the 24th to 26th December inclusive.

OAKWELL HALL
Birstall
West Yorkshire

Tel (0924) 474926

Open: Throughout the year, Monday to Saturday 10am to 5pm, Sunday 1pm to 5pm.

THE RED HOUSE
'Gomersal
West Yorkshire

Tel (0274) 872165

Open: Normally it is open to the public but recently it has been undergoing structural repairs and is likely to be reopened some time in 1989.

EPWORTH OLD RECTORY
Epworth
Nr Doncaster

Tel (0427) 872268

Open: Usual hours for visitors are from 10am to noon and from 2pm to 4pm.

CONISBROUGH CASTLE
Conisbrough
Nr Rotherham

Tel (0709) 863329

Open: From 9.30am, though closing times vary with the season.

RUSKIN GALLERY
Norfolk Street
Sheffield

Tel (0742) 734781

Open: Every day with the exception of Sundays.

Some Useful Addresses

THE W H AUDEN SOCIETY

Kathleen Bell
Flat 5, The Adage
86-88 High Street
Bidford-on-Avon
Via Alcester
Warwickshire
B50 4AD

THE SABINE BARING-GOULD SOCIETY

Rev D P R Shacklock
Holy Trinity Vicarage
2 Carlton Road
Redhill
Surrey
RH1 2BX

THE BRONTË SOCIETY

The Secretary: Mrs E Skirrow
The Brontë Parsonage Museum
Haworth
Keighley
BD22 8DR

DARESBURY LEWIS CARROLL SOCIETY

Kenneth L Oultram
Clatterwick Hall
Little Leigh
Northwich
Cheshire
CW8 4RJ

THE CHESTERTON SOCIETY

Paul Pinto
20 Valleyside
Hemel Hempstead
Herts
HP1 2LN

THE DRACULA SOCIETY

Hon Secretary: Robert James Leak
36 Wellington Street
Woolwich
London
SW18 6QF

THE DICKENS FELLOWSHIP

Alan S Watts
The Dickens House
48 Doughty Street
London
WC1N 2LF

There are also branches of the Dickens Fellowship in York and Sheffield.

THE GASKELL SOCIETY

Hon Secretary: Joan Leach
Far Yew Tree House
Over Tabley
Knutsford
Cheshire
WA16 0HN

THE WINIFRED HOLTBY COMMITTEE

John Markham
24 Wylies Road
Beverley
North Humberside
HU17 7AP

THE JOHNSON SOCIETY OF LONDON

Miss S P S Pigrome
Round Chimney
Playden
Rye
East Sussex
TN31 7UR

There is also a Johnson Society in Lichfield, c/o The Guildhall, Lichfield, Staffordshire.

THE FRIENDS OF SHANDY HALL

Mrs Julia Monkman
The Laurence Sterne Trust
Shandy Hall
Coxwold
York
YO6 4AD

THE TENNYSON SOCIETY

Miss K Jefferson ALA
Central Library
Free School Lane
Lincoln
LN2 1EZ

THE WALMSLEY SOCIETY

Founder/Secretary: Jack Hazell
47 Westcroft
Leominster
Hertfordshire
HR6 8HF

Membership Secretary: Miss Jane Ellis
152 Osmondthorpe Lane
Leeds
LS9 9EG

THE WORDSWORTH TRUST

Dove Cottage
Grasmere
Cumbria
LA22 9SH

A Brief Bibliography

Armstrong, Thomas. 'An Author Does Some Town Planning' (article in the *Bookseller,* 7th June 1947).

Atkins, John. *J B Priestley: Last of the Sages* (1981).

Baring-Gould, Sabine. *Yorkshire Oddities* (1874).

Bentley, Phyllis. *O Dreams, O Destinations* (1962).

Bishop, Alan (ed). *Chronicles of Friendship: Diaries of the Thirties* (1986).

Braine, John. *J B Priestley* (1979).

Brittain, Vera. *Testament of Friendship* (1940).

Cecil, Lord David. *Two Quiet Lives* (1948).

Defoe, Daniel. *Tour Through the Whole Island of Great Britain* (three volumes 1724-26; four volumes 1748).

Elliott, Ebenezer. *The Vernal Walk* (1789).

Emerson, R W. *Essays* (first series 1841, second series 1844).

Farnill, Barry. *Robin Hood's Bay* (1966).

Fletcher, J S. *Poems Chiefly Against Pessimism* (1893).

      ,   . *A Picturesque History of Yorkshire* (three volumes 1899-1901).

Fletcher, J S. *Collected Verse* (1931).

Fiennes, Celia. *The Journeys of Celia Fiennes* (ed Christopher Morris, 1947).

Gaskell, Elizabeth. *The Life of Charlotte Brontë* (1857).

Gray, Thomas. *Journal* (1775).

Hawthorne, Julian. *Hawthorne and his Circle* (1903).

Hawthorne, Nathaniel. *Our Old Home and English Notebooks* (1883).

Hutchinson, Alan. 'E C Booth: A Novelist of the Yorkshire Wolds' (article in the *Dalesman,* January 1955).

Jacobs, Naomi. *Me and the Swans* (1963).

Jameson, Storm. *Journey From the North* (two volumes 1969).

Larkin, Philip (ed). *The Oxford of Twentieth Century English Verse* (1973).

Lock, John, & Dixon, W T. *The Life, Letters and Times of the Rev Patrick Brontë* (1965).

Lockhart, J G. *Memoirs of the Life of Walter Scott* (1837-8).

Mackenzie, Sir Compton. *My Life and Times* (ten volumes, 1963-71).

Milford, Humphrey. *The Pageant of English Poetry* (1914).

Morton, H V. *The Call of England* (1928).

Priestley, J B. *English Journey* (1934).

    ,,   , ,, . *Margin Released* (1962).

Purcell, William. *Onward Christian Soldier: A Biography of Sabine Baring-Gould* (1957).

Purvis, Canon J S (ed). *The York Cycle of Mystery Plays in Modern English* (1957).

Ransome, Arthur. *The Autobiography of Arthur Ransome* (ed Rupert Hart-Davis, 1976).

Ratcliffe, Dorothy Una. *Cranesbill Caravan* (1961).

Read, Sir Herbert. *The Innocent Eye* (1933).

    ,, , ,,   ,,   *The Contrary Experience* (1963).

Riley, William. *Sunset Reflection* (1967).

Ruskin, John. *Praeterita* (1886-8).

Sadleir, Michael. *Trollope: A Commentary* (1928, revised 1945).

Sitwell, Sir Osbert. *Left Hand, Right Hand* (1945).

    ,, , ,,   ,, . *The Scarlet Tree* (1946).

    ,, , ,,   ,, . *Great Morning* (1948).

Spring, Howard. *Heaven Lies About Us* (1939).

    ,, ,   ,, . *In the Meantime* (1942).

    ,, ,   ,, . *And Another Thing* (1946).

Sutcliffe, Halliwell. *The Striding Dales* (1929).

Trollope, Anthony. *Autobiography* (1883).

Turner, J Horsfall. *Haworth Past and Present* (1897).

Turner, Whiteley. *A Springtime Saunter Round and About Brontëland* (1913).

Walmsley, Leo. *Love in the Sun* (1939).

    ,,   , ,, . *So Many Loves* (1944).

    ,,   , ,, . *The Golden Waterwheel* (1954).

Walmsley, Leo. *Paradise Creek* (1963).

Watkins, John. *The Life, Poetry and Letters of Ebenezer Elliott* (1850).

Watson, William. *Collected Poems* (1904).

Wenham, Leslie. *The History of Richmond School* (1957).

Wesley, John. *Journals 1735-1781.*

Photographic Acknowledgements

Paul Berry, p37 p42 (top): Black Swan Hotel, p68 (top); *Bradford Telegraph and Argus,* p115, 118, 130; Brontë Society, 42-3 (Anne Brontë), 110 (top), 111 (top and bottom), 114 (top and bottom); Dorothy Burrows, p106 (top and bottom); Castle Howard Estates, p19 (bottom); Rev Richard Cooper, p76, 77; *Dalesman,* p31 (bottom); Dracula Society, p63; English Heritage, p144 (bottom); Gary Firth, p119; Michael Fryer, p69; Hull City Council, p30, 31; Hull City Museums, p28; Hull Univeristy Brynmor Jones Library, p36; Jim Jarratt, p96 (top and bottom); Kirklees Metropolitan Council: Libraries, Museums and Arts, p110 (bottom); Laurence Sterne Trust, p11 (top and bottom); Manchester University John Rylands Library, p54; M T D Rigg Publications, p107 (top and bottom); National Portrait Gallery, p10 (bottom, reproduced courtesy of the Laurence Sterne Trust), 18; North Yorkshire County Libraries, p42 (bottom), 43; Rotherham Council: Libraries, Museums and Arts, p145; Ruskin Gallery, p150, 151; Scarborough Tourist Board, p43 (Anne Brontë's grave); Raresby Sitwell, p46; Skipton Libraries, p84 (top and bottom); Fred Spencer, p1, 2 (bottom), 29 (bottom), 31 (top), 85 (top); Stephen Joseph Theatre-in-the-Round, p47; Sutcliffe Gallery, p51 (top and bottom); Wakefield Historical Publications, p131 (bottom); Richard Walton, p131 (top); *Whitby Gazette,* p62; Peter Woods, p50; York City Art Gallery, p10 (top), 19 (top), 24 (top), 25; *Yorkshire Evening Press,* p2 (top), 3; *Yorkshire Post,* p97.

Index